D1827495

Major Airports of the World

Major Airports of the World

Roy Allen

LONDON

IAN ALLAN LTD

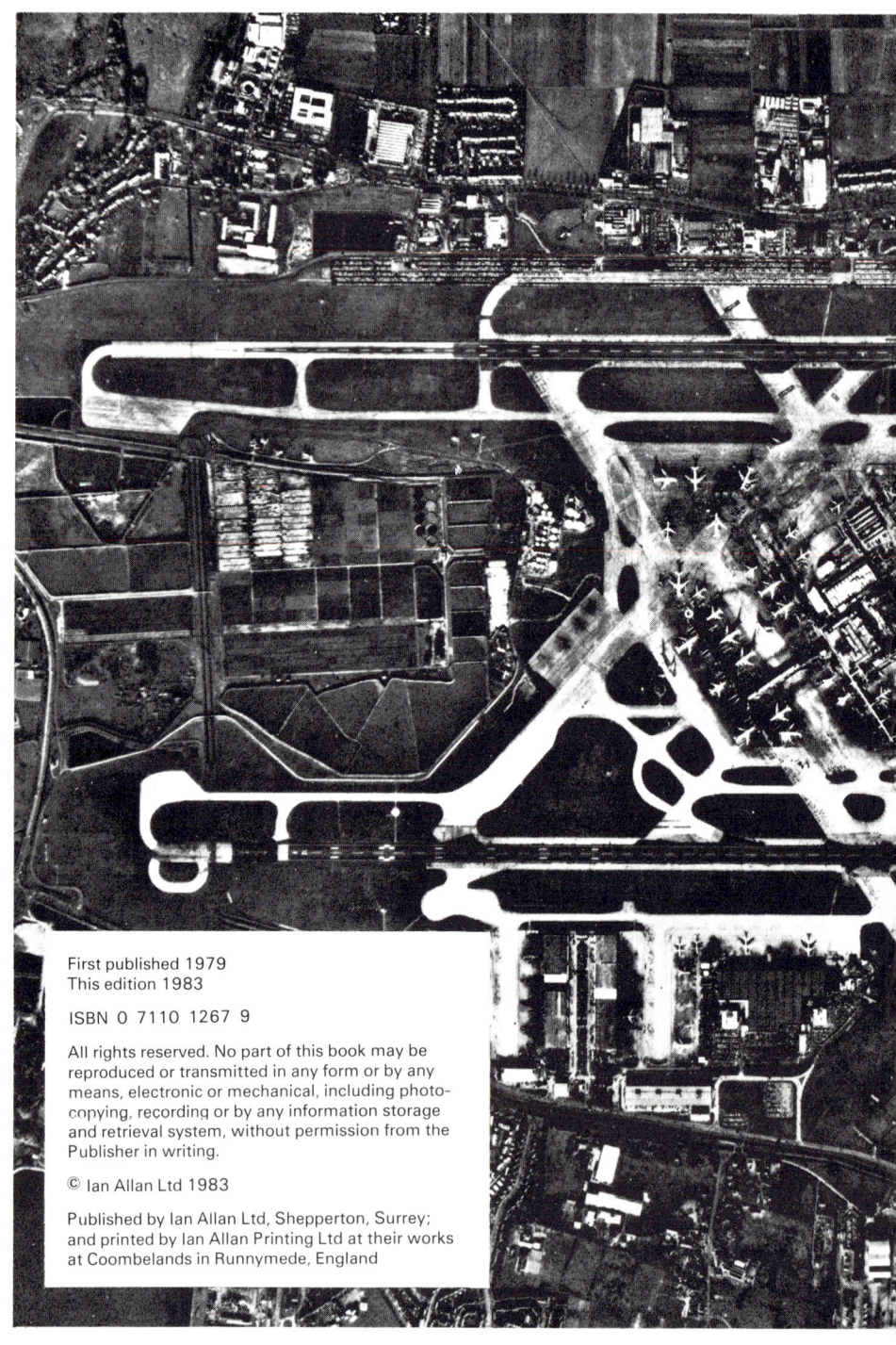

First published 1979
This edition 1983

ISBN 0 7110 1267 9

© Ian Allan Ltd 1983

Published by Ian Allan Ltd, Shepperton, Surrey;
and printed by Ian Allan Printing Ltd at their works
at Coombelands in Runnymede, England

Contents

Front cover: *Bahrain International.*

Back cover, top: *Amsterdam (Schiphol).*

Back cover, centre: *London (Heathrow).*

Back cover, bottom: *Kansas City International.*

Left: *London (Heathrow).*

Introduction

The international airport scene has been marked by a number of dramatic developments in the four years since publication of my last edition of this book, among them a catastrophic decline in the fortunes of the world's airlines, resulting in a consequent decline in the number of air transport movements at international airports, and sometimes dramatic falls in the volumes of cargo handled at the airports.

The security position appears to worsen yearly at airports, as terrorists of various inclinations or political motives make their presence felt; Stansted Airport, England was the subject of one dramatic end to an airliner hijacking recently, when only the practised efficiency of the British police and airport staff saw a closure of the incident with no casualties.

As an economic depression has passed around the world, airline revenues have fallen sharply, and airliner cancellations have replaced the great surge of orders which were witnessed in the 1978-1980 period, with a consequent impact made upon aircraft manufacturers. Lockheed terminated production of their Rolls-Royce-powered TriStar airliner, and McDonnell Douglas as good as gave up production of the DC-10, while the production line was kept intact. Airbus Industrie continued to do well, although the dramatic collapse of Laker Airways with debts of £260 million in 1982 did not help the Airbus consortium, which had to re-sell Laker's 10 Airbuses. Even the Boeing Airplane Company was obliged to defer delivery of many of its new, fuel-efficient and quieter Boeing 757 and B767 aircraft until airlines were once again able to take them into their fleets.

Seattle-Tacoma Airport is a prime facility for travellers from Washington State and also Western Canada, because of the wide range of services available for passengers. Note satellite terminals on either side of the main terminal.

The world's international airports have shouldered the burden of these problems, and while much loss of income has been experienced in many quarters as a result of the depressed market, there has at least been a pause in the development work which has until recently appeared to be never-ending, and some airports have actually been glad of the breathing space. Many airports have taken the opportunity with the pause in traffic growth to complete existing schemes in the confidence that they will not be outdated so quickly, and also give a reappraisal of their airport's needs for the future.

Traffic forecasting, always a difficult exercise, and subject to constant revision, has been looked at afresh, and more realistic projections made for the next five years and sometimes to the end of the century.

In this revised and expanded edition of *Major Airports of the World*, recent developments and the plans in hand for the immediate and longer-term future at some 93 principal airports are described — underlining the fact that, in spite of depressions in the air transport industry, airport authorities hold full confidence in the future. One has only to look at the debate that has ensued over the plans for a new airport for London, and the energy with which the replacement airport for Hong Kong's Kai Tak Airport is being pursued, to be made aware of the continued importance of the world's airports.

International air transport is a resilient industry and an adaptive one, and the world's airports are demonstrating increasing professionalism in adapting to suit air transport's changing needs, as the following pages bear out. Air transport is also a fascinating business with an important end purpose, and this too is clear from the airport stories which follow.

Roy Allen

Part One

Airport Types and their Location

As the photographs in this book show, the airports of the world have come a very long way from the grass fields with a few simple markers which characterised the start of air transport 60 years ago. Indeed, the international airport business has become an exact science, bringing into play a whole range of disciplines and equipments including electronics, mechanical systems, audio and visual communications, traffic management, transport planning and fuel handling, as well as Customs procedures, cargo processing and 'people-moving'. The airport terminal, and its related buildings, is the hub of all this activity, and in thinking of airports we naturally tend to think of this as the airport itself.

By way of establishing the various types of airport in use around the world, however, it is instructive to classify them and look at the various categories they fall under. This has nothing to do with terminal design or runway layout, which are planning matters, but, rather, airport types, of which there are a number.

They include the all-grass, the land-based and the water-based airports of which the latter is similar to but not the same as the offshore type. Variations of these include the grass and concrete airport, that is, the grass airfield equipped with one or more concrete runway, the all-concrete airport, and the floating airport, which has been an interesting concept of recent years.

Prague Airport seen from the airside. Large numbers of the user-aircraft are, inevitably, Russian-made.

These airports will fall into different categories which indicate their operational function, such as regional, major international, general aviation and satellite etc. The term is not generally used in Britain but in the USA there are 'hub' airports and these are classified as large, medium and small according to the number of communities the airports serve: a non-hub airport is one which sees the embarkation annually of less than 0.05% of the national total of airline passengers.

There are charter airports and transit airports, although neither of these are specific categories but have come to be so classed because of the nature of their operations. The charter airport, for example, has come to be known by this term because the bulk of its traffic is inclusive tour or charter traffic and its facilities are geared to this type of operation (as Luton, for example, in the UK). Likewise, the transit airport is not a specific class, but it will be found in many countries handling a preponderance of transit traffic. In this regard it is interesting to know that Athens Airport was rated in 1975 by the Hellenic Civil Aviation Authority as the busiest transit airport among 36 of the world's international airports, the explanation being that Athens serves as a connecting point for so many international flights. Equally, Athens is a busy scheduled-traffic airport.

The regional airport serves, as it suggests, various regions with the bulk of its traffic, while the satellite airport is one which serves as a feeder airport to the nearby major facility, often a principal international hub, such as New York's John F. Kennedy International Airport. The satellite airport often serves as an 'overflow' and diversion airport for the main international facility, from which it is sometimes found expedient to divert flights because of weather problems or traffic congestion. The British Government incidentally, proposed four new categories of airport in England and Wales with its master plan for the development of the nation's

airports up to 1990. These were: Gateway international airports; Regional airports, to serve as a second tier and catering mainly for UK domestic, international short-haul and charter services; Local airports, which would cater mainly for local needs; and General aviation airports, a type of facility well known in some countries like the USA, but which has been almost non-existent up to now in Britain.

There are heliports and seaplane bases, particularly in the USA, where in 28 states there are some 620, many offering channel navigational lights and fuelling, restaurant and other facilities. The heliport is licensed for helicopter operations and is in a class of its own insofar as it excludes fixed-wing aircraft. There are few purpose-built heliports in the United Kingdom, but this number is likely to grow as private business flying increases yearly and the prospect of international services by public carriers using helicopters becomes a real probability.

Airline operations do not take place on any scale from all-grass airports, but there are some of these airfields still endearing themselves to the hearts of visitors, notably in the UK, where new civil operators continue to launch themselves into business in spite of the odds against them. Pleasant country fields, such as Sywell Airport, Northamptonshire, play their part in making these starts possible at relatively little cost.

One of the first airlines in the world to carry freight, KLM Royal Dutch Airlines makes a big business of this still, with a large fleet of Combi B747s. This is a palletised load being moved into the cabin on a powered, roller track.

In distinct contrast and becoming known as the most promising types for the future are the water-based airports, which have their own runways and a portion of their terminal facilities built adjoining or actually over water. A large number of this type of airport has been proposed in recent years, among them the now defunct Maplin project, which would have been partly built on land reclaimed from the sea, and the most recent Changi Airport, Singapore, which is now operational. These provide for massive passenger terminal complexes and long runway systems to handle international traffic. As land becomes scarce and expensive the coastal or water-based airport has much to offer, for it has environmental attractions too, with minimum aircraft noise and little pollution. Sydney, Honolulu, Changi, Kiushu in Japan, Haugesund in Norway, Rio de Janeiro and Nice are all airport locations on or adjoining the sea developed in the last few years.

Taking this concept a stage further, although without much progress so far, is the true island airport, which is literally planned as a floating offshore airport. This type has been proposed as a completely man-made structure, anchored some way off the coast from the city the airport is intended to serve, and bearing runways, passenger terminals and all administration blocks. The island airport is linked to the land by a causeway, which would carry a high speed train service for passengers and personnel.

If one adds to all of these the much talked of all-cargo airport, which is sometimes regarded as attractive but generally agreed to be a commercial non-starter, the number of categories and types of airport is seen as substantial. There may even be more in the future.

Airport Design

While the different types of airport in use stem largely from air transport evolution, airport design has been given close attention in the past 25 years and in the past 15 it has become something of a scientific study.

Everybody knew — or thought they knew — when hard runway airports began to be built that operators required at least one runway facing into wind, and another for operations in the next most likely wind direction. This thinking was followed by a period which saw multi-runway patterns, appearing to take care of all such problems; then aircraft weights and performances became such as to make runway numbers and bearing strengths practically immaterial, with only the runway length appearing to matter. It is interesting in this regard to listen to the arguments about Gatwick Airport today, where, for largely environmental reasons, its operators maintain that it will never need a second runway to handle the traffic that is proposed for it. 25 years ago, when it was re-built to a Stage 2 development plan, land was earmarked for a second, parallel runway at Gatwick as a matter of course, as plans show, with the only uncertainty about this runway being the precise date when it would be required.

Considerations over runway arrangement today have changed as aircraft have become more advanced, and design has come to be centred upon operational requirements, with new factors playing a part. Thus, an airport built to have more than one runway will most likely be designed with a view to multiple take-offs and landings, and the runways therefore arranged in parallel. Dallas/Fort Worth

Airport and Narita, Tokyo, are typical examples of this thinking, with the American airport not even really having to bother about the other prime factor which influences airport design today — noise.

This has become a planning matter, with airport authorities in constant debate with aircraft constructors as they try to resolve air transport's requirements for the future. The quieter aircraft that are coming, however, will be joined by shorter take-off and landing aircraft, and this will have its effect upon airport design. With future transport aircraft, runway lengths common today could be halved, and a new and safe era of operations could begin.

In looking at airport design today, planners consider in particular operational requirements and the economic aspect of the whole facility, and consequently design characteristics derive from these. While the airport is still something of a showplace, its parallel runway system will have been incorporated in order to maximise the number of take-offs and landings during a working year and thereby get the best value from what is a very expensive undertaking. Likewise, the actual lengths of runways laid down will have been dictated by the runway requirements of contemporary aircraft, and up until recently these have been 10,000ft and more (two of the runways at Dallas/Fort Worth are 11,400ft long).

The demand for such incredible amounts of runway space imposed strains upon localities which became too much to bear in certain places, among

Otherwise known as Sea-Tac, the Washington State airport is big and busy, and equipped with a sophisticated rapid transit system

The passenger loading bridge, airbridge or Aerobridge, was one of the inspired developments brought by the jet age, which saw a mass traffic, and which could not be walked about airport aprons in the wet or snow.

them London and New York which were both glad to find unnecessary the need to construct additional international airports when forecasts signified a slowing down in growth. When a third London airport has to be built it will be interesting to see how aircraft performance has changed its specification.

In looking at terminal design, planners are caught today between creating attractive, and sometimes grandiose, structures and purely functional facilities where a prime consideration is handling an impressive annual traffic throughput. In this difficult task they generally do a good job, for there are so many factors to take into account now as it is recognised, finally, that air travel is just one element in an integrated transport system, rather than being a special means of moving about the world.

With airport terminal design the planner has to look at passenger throughput at peak times and provide enough space to allow for large numbers of passengers. Equally, he has to consider the off-peak periods and the amount of money under-utilised space can cost authorities. As an example, the first stage passenger terminal at Narita Airport handles a maximum of 3,200 departing and arriving passengers an hour in the peak periods, which had to be equated with terminal costs; in total, Narita cost $793 million.

Then again, the planner has to consider the place of the airport in the total traffic scene. Is it intended to be, for example, a replacement airport for a city, as

Charles de Gaulle Airport was for Le Bourget? With such knowledge in mind the planners of the Paris Airport Authority were aware that Roissy had to be large, capable of substantial expansion up to the end of the century, and equipped with the most modern systems of transporting travellers while on the ground and between their aeroplanes — the reason for which they were there in the first place. Equally, the PAA planners knew that, as the airport for the capital city of France, Charles de Gaulle Airport had to be astride main road and rail arteries. In its finished, unlovely rough-concrete form, CDG Airport may not be attractive to the visitor, but it does fulfil its role.

The terminal design at Roissy represents one approach to handling the passenger. Travellers are separated and channelled according to their flight to one of seven satellite terminals surrounding a main structure ('the Aerogare'). This satellite concept had been employed previously at Toronto and Geneva, and elsewhere. At Toronto for a variety of reasons it failed, while at Geneva it has been a success. Other airports, such as London's Heathrow, employ other design ideas, such as taking the traveller up one or more levels above the ground in his passage through the terminal, and then back down to the ground on the airside in order for him to board the aircraft.

If such planning ideas do not work or seem poor ideas, they have to be numbered among the many considerations requiring much thought, including baggage handling and flow, private car movement and accommodation, provision for invalids, large numbers of buses, delayed aircraft, with their prospect of parties of passengers, and the provision for airport and airline administrative functions and, perhaps, the most important matter of all, eating and drinking.

Running the Airport

Inevitably, airport administration has become more bureaucratic over the years, but this is not a criticism; rather it is a comment upon the remarkable development of a system which could not be left to untrained managers and demanded the professional touch of highly qualified men and organisations to cover every aspect.

There are not many airports about the world now that handle commercial air services without some degree of governmental involvement, for if an airport is privately owned it will almost certainly have ATC services provided by a government body, and it is more than likely that government finance will be provided to help run the airport. An airport handling air carrier services is part of a system which now stretches around the world, and for this reason local and central government bodies have become involved and various airport professional organisations tied in.

Airport ownership and administration is readily classified. Air transport airports are owned by local authorities, such as municipalities, towns or states, by the government of the country in which they are located, or by autonomous operating bodies which have been established by the government and local authorities between them or by the government alone: relatively few are privately owned.

In the United Kingdom a number of the regional airports are owned by local councils or authorities — typical examples are Manchester, Luton, Liverpool and Birmingham. East Midlands Airport is owned by an authority made up of the Derbyshire, Leicestershire and Nottingham county councils. The matching arrangement in the USA might be typified by Baltimore-Washington Airport, which is owned by the State of Maryland.

Government-owned airports are the most common, and in Britain these are represented by the airports operated by the British Airports Authority, which was established by the Government under an Act of Parliament as an autonomous owning and operating body. The BAA is otherwise a nationalised concern responsible to the Government. In other parts of the world, ranging from the Middle East to Africa and South America, the state is the sole owner and operator of airports in particular countries.

A development in more recent years, which is seen increasingly, is the BAA-type of autonomous owner/operator. This type of undertaking can be found in India, where the IAAI is responsible for the major gateways of Bombay, Delhi, Calcutta and Madras; in Denmark, in the form of the Copenhagen Airports Authority, and in Holland, where the Amsterdam Airport Authority is responsible for Schiphol. There are many more, and a recently established Authority has been that for Curacao Airport, in the Netherlands Antilles, which has been created to free the airport from direct government operation.

At Schiphol, however, as at Frankfurt and Cologne, the state is a partner in the ownership of the airport rather than its sole controller, for the airport authority has been established as a company

and, in the case of Amsterdam's airport, the shareholders in this company are the State of the Netherlands, the Municipality of Amsterdam and the Municipality of Rotterdam. Flughafen Frankfurt AG has principal shareholders in the Federal German Government, the State of Hesse, and the city of Frankfurt am Main. Likewise Cologne-Bonn Airport operates as a company, whose principal shareholder is the Federal Republic which shares responsibility with the Land of North Rhine-Westphalia and the city of Cologne.

The running of the world's airports is often the province of organisations other than the state or the appointed airport authority, for this is a specialised task, and one in which Britain has been particularly skilled. In overseas locations such as the Middle East and Africa it is quite common, therefore, to find airports in states such as Dubai and Abu Dhabi, in the United Arab Emirates, and Swaziland under the management of British companies like International Aeradio, whose services and skills have ranged from supplying and installing the air traffic control consoles and related equipment, to providing ATC and management personnel to handle the complete tasks of administration. At Southall, Middlesex, the headquarters of IAL conducts training courses for the nationals of these countries to ultimately assume responsibility for the airport operational tasks.

In the planning of airports, government bodies play a central role today, as might be expected, for there are so many issues which require the overseeing of government departments, such as surface transport infrastructure, environmental disturbance and, of course, safety. There are also the matters of international telecommunications and the airways system, and the government must have final authority over these. Because the whole airport system is now so complex, however, various specialised organisations and bodies with special skills have come to make important contributions to the industry, and these range from the airport divisions of associations such as ICAO and IATA to the 'trouble-shooting' councils such as ICAA, AOCI and the WEAA.

These last are essentially airport associations, whose members meet regularly to discuss developments of mutual interest and report on various ideas, such as with the Paris-based International Civil Airports Association and the Washington-based Airport Operators Council International. Such bodies are often the medium through which airport-users' interests are made known and effected to the betterment of air transport generally and for the users in particular — which include government planners and administrators as well as the airlines and general passengers at large.

Passenger Facilities and Amenities

One of the reasons why air travel has taken over from surface transport as the means by which people travel today is its simple attraction of being advanced in every respect. In Victorian times, when railway travel was a brand new experience, the equipment and facilities were doubtless breathtaking to the travellers of the time, and in the supersonic era air transport is similarly awe-inspiring, pleasurable, and remarkable in its achievement for the passenger.

The airport is the hub of the operation, and it might be said to be the railway terminal of the jet age, for as air transport continues to move forward at a steady pace, enlargements and further improvements to existing facilities are made, and these in turn seem to attract yet more traffic.

There is not doubt whatever that the aircraft and the airports have been greatly responsible for the fantastic volumes of traffic that are moved today, for as a result of the constantly made improvements the international airport has generally become a comfortable and entertaining place, as well as one holding tremendous interest and excitement. Where else, for example, can one always find a great number of people of different nationalities gathered together except at the airport? Where else can one have a fine meal and be given an aerial show at the same time but at the airport restaurant? For the

The transportation of large numbers of people at airports is a major problem for authorities, many of whom have resorted to continually-running tracked cars — as here at Dallas-Fort Worth — to get people to their proper terminal. The cost of running these systems is offset against the airports' general operational costs.

Airlines generally do an excellent job of transporting passengers' luggage and linking it with them on arrival. Pilferage will probably always be a problem, however, for the pieces pass through many hands.

person interested in languages, aeroplanes, technical devices and ideas, foreign countries and pretty girls, the airport is probably the best place in the land.

The true commercialisation of airport services occurred first in the home of air transport, the USA, when it was recognised that the provision of a variety of attractions could bring in more money than that required solely to provide for the passengers. With the moneys from concessions and a variety of rents, the operating authorities gained revenue to help pay for their airports and fund development schemes, and in due course this became the accepted routine.

From such moves the world has gained a whole range of airport services, from the snack bars to a range of restaurants, airport hotels, motels, cinemas, hairdressing facilities, florists, sauna baths and showers, banks, hire car services, bookstalls and gift shops, airport museums, spectators' galleries, and, of course, the duty-free shop. All of these facilities are in the best interests of travellers and have done much to swell the numbers of people flying, although it might be thought that things have reached a curious state when 50% of the British Airports Authority's revenue now comes from rents and such concessions.

It must be acknowledged that the BAA has been a leader in the provision of some services for passengers at its airports, however, among them lifts, inclined ramps and special toilets for disabled travellers, and first-aid rooms and medical services,

13

flight		from	last stop
SA	223	JOHANNESBURG	
BA	931	SYDNEY	BAHRAIN
AR	132	BUENOS AIRES	PARIS
BA	811	DELHI	BEIRUT
TW	701	FRANKFURT	
GF	009	MUSCAT	BEIRUT
PK	781	KARACHI	PARIS
ME	203	BEIRUT	
PA	001	DELH	FRANKFURT
ET	706	ADD ABABA	ATHENS
SV	783	DHA N	ROME
JL	1407	TOK	ANCHORAGE

Electronic information display boards provide clear facts for the traveller, say all that is generally needed, and obviate the constant noise of audible information relays — which most people ignore or cannot properly hear. The gentleman appears to prefer the semaphore method.

One of the important aspects of air transport is Facilitation, which quite simply covers ways of improving and speeding passenger flow through airports. One such way discussed for some time is the credit card type passport, which might speed passenger processing. On the reverse side of the card information printed on horizontal magnetic strips can allow electronic recording of entry control data.

as well as restrooms for mothers with small children.

Moving walkways are now features of most big airports, and these devices, sometimes called travelators, Speedwalks or moving pavements, take a lot of the effort out of reaching the holding lounges disposed around or at the end of the piers. The one criticism that might be made of these is that they are rarely long enough and far too few in number.

As airports get busier some facilities are introduced to answer a need while others, regrettably, disappear because of new pressures of fresh thinking. Heathrow saw the opening of an underground rail link in December 1977, which makes it possible for passengers to journey right through from Piccadilly Circus to the heart of the airport with their baggage and without changing

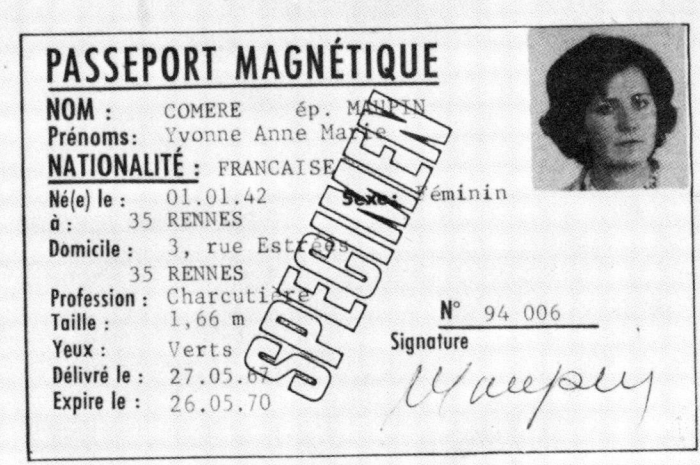

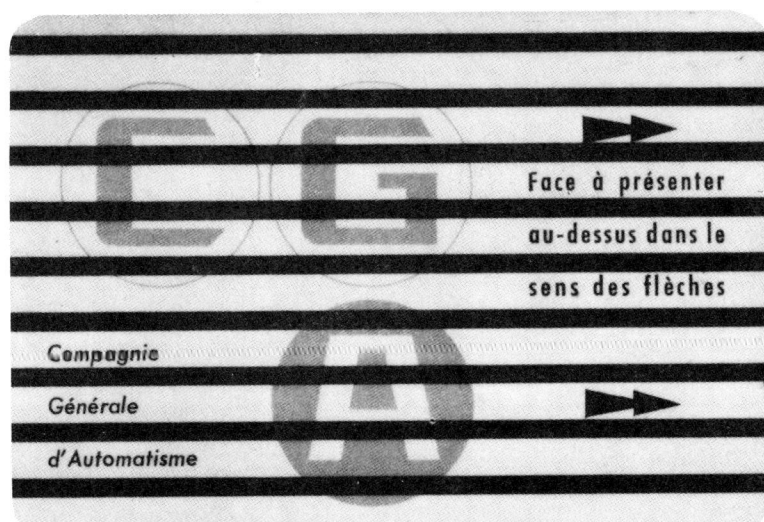

Gothenburg, Sweden, introduced a smart new airport just a few years ago, to serve the country's west coast cities and ports. As with many airports, the heaviest traffic is at peak times, and much of the airport's day is otherwise deceptively quiet.

Baggage handling is one of the bigger air transport operations, and missing baggage is often laid at the door of the airport authorities, — who more often than not safely hold the lost item until tracked down. This baggage transporter is at Johannesburg Airport.

trains, and this service is expected to be used by a substantial proportion of the airport's users before long. While nothing to do with the airport authority, the check-in facility at the West London Air Terminal was closed beforehand, thus denying passengers the chance of disposing of their baggage to the airlines before reaching the congested halls and check-in counters of Heathrow. For the many travellers who use them, bus services continue to run between the airport and this London terminal — but checking in has to be done at the airport.

At Heathrow and many other airports about the world, the demands of airport security have made their impression upon the rooftop spectators' galleries, and at some international airports these important places are now sadly closed altogether, to be re-opened, perhaps, at happier, unspecified dates in the future. Such places are important to air transport, for apart from providing a point from which a departing relative or friend's aircraft can be watched, the galleries represent the freedom implicit in air transport. Moreover, the airport is usually partly paid for by the taxpayer, who should not be denied the small, sometimes emotional, pleasure of watching an aircraft departure.

Among the numerous facilities for travellers at the airports of the world are car parks — computer-controlled in some places, such as Charles de Gaulle Airport, Paris, while scant in number at others — churches and chapels, which contribute nothing towards airport revenues but much towards some travellers' spiritual tranquility, and intra-airport

The duty free airport shop has become a major attraction at the world's airports, and earns large sums of money for operators and concessionaires alike. Equally large sums are spent by travellers at airport shops generally, for a lot of the purchases are with leisure money.

transit systems, such as those in use at Seattle-Tacoma and Dallas-Fort Worth Airports, which carry passengers between terminals and other parts of the airport on continually running train systems.

Many of the basic services can be improved, such as baggage delivery and flight information, but new ideas such as Airtrans are coming into airports, and a lot more are promised.

17

Work on the Ground

The parties to ground activities at international airports are primarily the operators, that is the airlines, the airport management organisation itself, and numerous sub-contracting organisations which work for either of these parties. In the case of the airlines, the carriers are concerned with a range of tasks apart from the actual flying of the aeroplanes, ranging from shepherding the passengers on board to fuelling the aircraft and providing in-flight meals for the travellers, who can usually be said to have keen appetites. For the airlines, such services cover check-in and baggage handling, directing and guiding passengers through procedures required by the airport, monitoring the movements of groups (including charter parties), and co-ordinating the movement of these passengers with the ground handling of the aircraft for its task of transporting the passengers away to some other airport.

The majority of airlines perform their own passenger handling services at their national airports, and in some cases at overseas airports as well, but in some instances ground handling agencies perform this task for the carriers. In the UK

Once it was the humble tractor, and now it is the heavy duty Airtug which pushes — or pulls — big aircraft on to the ramp for take-off, thereby saving fuel, and also making less noise near the terminal.

one such ground handling agency is Servisair, while another is Gatwick Handling. In the Middle East the agency as Dubai Airport is the Dubai National Air Travel Agency, while at Bahrain the local passenger handling company is Bahrain Air Services. The existence of such companies has come about simply because the business of passenger handling has often become too big a task for individual airlines to cope with.

In scope and sheer volume it would be difficult to calculate the ratio of work done on the ground to that in the air, but an airline's fleet of surface vehicles will often far outnumber the number of aircraft in the carrier's fleet. The vehicles and equipments required for the surface tasks are multifarious. They include baggage conveyors, passenger buses, catering trucks, step units, air starters, crew vans, tractors or airtugs, forklifts, baggage dollies, toilet carts and ground power units. If an airline is essentially a cargo carrier its equipment fleet is likely to include cargo transporters, dollies, elevators, scissor lifts, container transfer vehicles, ULD transporters, mobile conveyors, trailers and forklifts.

Many of these vehicles or equipments may be owned by companies which serve the airlines, and a recent trend has seen the establishment of a number of organisations whose purpose in life has been to make available such equipments to airlines on a lease basis at airports in various parts of the world. One of the reasons for this is that the capital cost of the equipments concerned has become too great for

It is generally given slight regard by the traveller, but the matter of an airport fire requires constant vigilance and readiness by the appropriate airport organisation. This is the fire alarm console at Johannesburg Airport — whose duty officer has simply moved out of the way of the camera.

some airlines to purchase outright and in any quantity. For major airlines with sometimes as many as 80 outstations, however, there is little choice but to invest in their own substantial fleet of ground vehicles.

For the airport authorities the work on the ground is similarly as heavy in volume as that which it is controlling in the air, and airport authorities the world over equally have sizeable fleets of ground vehicles. These will range from motorised runway sweepers to passenger step units and airbridges, fire-fighting vehicles, administrative cars and airport passenger buses. Vehicles such as the 20,000-gallon fuellers usually belong to the oil companies, who like various other agencies, work for the airports under contract.

The many tasks of moving passengers through an airport are shared between the managing authority and the carriers with a number of other organisations playing their part. Customs and Immigration will, for example, be the responsibility of the national government agency, while likewise, Security will involve the services of the police — and in some countries even the Army. In some countries the task of bird-scaring is an important matter, and special organisations are employed by the airport specifically for this job. In the case of Security this has become a particular problem in the last 15 years, and different bodies have been varyingly made responsible for the matter, ranging from an airport's own police force to the airlines themselves. Terminal security is now generally regarded as the concern of the airport authority, while security on board the aircraft is the concern of the airlines.

The airport authority is responsible for baggage being moved through the airport which individual airlines may load and unload their own aircraft (and sometimes other airlines' too). Information dissemination in the terminals is the province of the airport authority, as is the provision of car parking facilities, restaurants and luggage repositories. Shops, taxi and car hire services, airport hotels, banks and the acutal operation of the restaurants will all be the responsibility of commerical undertakings who work within the airport for the end point of serving the passenger.

At an airport such as Heathrow this can involve more than 50,000 people, which is a measure of the importance of the airport today.

Tranquility in the Air

Every aid or device that is introduced to make flying safer and more efficient brings with it a penalty, in the form of fresh expense to the user and a further complication of the system. Thus, over the past 25 years we have seen in air transport the mandatory introduction of airborne flight recorders, anti-collision lights, triplicated hazard warning and remedial systems, high-definition radars and ground proximity warning systems. It can be said that air transport is the better for the employment of all of these devices, but they have brought a new measure of sophistication to a system in which technology is now said to be running ahead of practical use of the hardware.

Where operational aids are concerned, the airport is now the operator of a multitude of devices, ranging from terminal and airfield surface movement radars to selective calling systems and transmitters to Category IIIa ILS. Even before an airliner is ready for flight it will be under aerodrome control. When the passengers have boarded and the pilot signified readiness for flight, it will be the air traffic controllers at the airport who give him permission for movement away from the terminal and clearance for take-off. He will be directed by the airport to a specified flight level and monitored by airport radar while he is in the terminal area, and until he is handed over to en route air traffic control. At this point the originating airport's responsibilities end.

As he approaches the destination airport he will be observed on control centre radar, brought under the responsibility of approach control for landing, and closely monitored, both visually and audibly, until ground control indicate that the aircraft is at pierside and the flight ended.

The multitude of devices employed by the airport on the ground to facilitate the passage of 400 ton aircraft carrying upwards of 450 passengers is likewise vast, and includes airfield surface movement radars, runway visual range measures (RVR), taxiway and runway lighting systems, and their complementary aids, the visual approach slope indicators (VASI). Coupled with these are the instrument landing systems which, brought to a high degree of perfection with Autoland, enable aircraft to take-off and land in zero-visibility conditions. The latest follow-on to this last equipment is the microwave landing system (MLS) and which overcomes the clutter and interference experienced with the more basic ILS and which will permit

Birmingham Airport now has a new airport terminal and will shortly have the first magnetic levitation-driven rapid transit system for connecting passengers to the terminal. The whole scene is watched over from the control tower, seen here.

multipath approaches. The American-devised Time Reference Scanning Beam system of MLS was selected by ICAO in 1978 as the best type to replace existing ILS systems in the 1980s and is now being manufactured for international installation.

The world of air transport has many imperfections, and unfortunately there are still many international airports whose equipment is below the best standards. An airliner taking off from an airport equipped with the very best aids, such as at Heathrow, may well find, therefore, that it is bound for some airport whose basic instrument landing system has not progressed beyond Category II, while its runway lighting system is far from comprehensive. Cost is a factor here, for airport authorities in some countries may have budgets which are slim by comparison with those of wealthier air-faring nations.

In this regard the United Nationas agency, ICAO, performs a valuable task through its airport development programmes, which have enabled many airports to be brought up to standards which they might otherwise not have met for the supersonic age. IATA, too has made its contribution to the development of less well-equipped airports, both in their planning and management.

For the future, more aids and devices will be required and will be installed at the world's airports to meet the needs of a business which is daily seeing more airliners in the air and calling for high-speed reactions on the part of pilots. With supersonic airliners amongst these aircraft the margin for error is narrowing.

In spite of the fact that the world civil aviation fleet has gone up from under 3,000 aircraft in 1946 to over 9,000 in 1981, air transport is, nevertheless, becoming safer in statistical terms every day.

From its humble beginnings, 64 years ago, air transport has become not only a highly attractive medium of travel but a safe one, and it is not surprising therefore that the world's airports have blossomed into the remarkable places that they are today, as the following pages illustrate.

Approach control radar being watched closely by the Belgian National Airways' controller at Brussels National Airport.

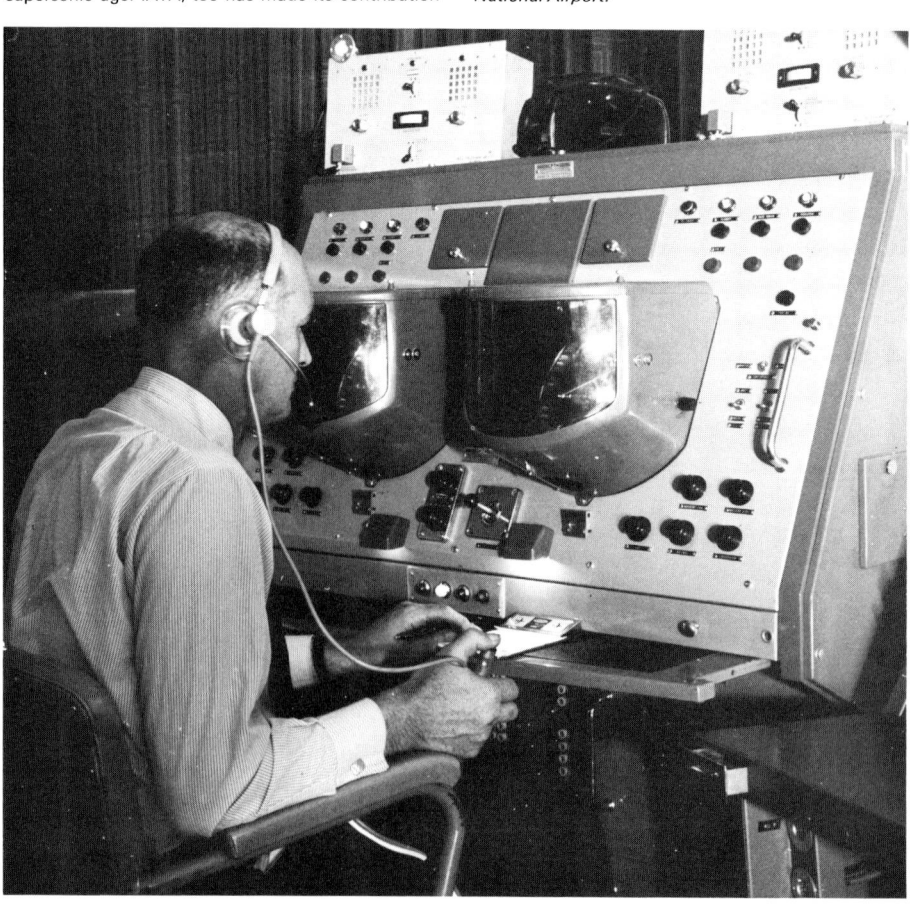

Part Two
Statistics

Major Airports of the World: Ranking by Traffic Volume, 1981

Ranking	Airport	Number of passengers in 000s
1	Chicago O'Hare	37,976
2	Atlanta	37,594
3	Los Angeles	32,722
4	London Heathrow	26,400
5	New York JFK	25,752
6	Dallas/Fort Worth	23,533
7	Denver	22,601
8	Tokyo Haneda	21,235
9	Miami	19,848·6
10	San Francisco	19,848·5
11	New York La Guardia	18,146
12	Osaka	17,087
13	Paris Orly	17,012
14	Frankfurt	16,953
15	Boston	14,827
16	Toronto	14,512
17	Honolulu	14,344
18	Washington National	14,175
19	Mexico City	12,780
20	Houston	11,601

Major Airports of the World: Ranking by Air Transport Movements, 1981

Ranking	Airport	Number
1	Chicago O'Hare	554,500
2	Atlanta	523,100
3	Dallas/Fort Worth	445,800
4	Los Angeles	380,200
5	Denver	379,300
6	Pittsburgh	320,400
7	St Louis	302,600
8	Miami	265,700
9	San Francisco	262,600
10	Philadelphia	255,600
11	Boston	251,600
12	London Heathrow	247,100
13	New York JFK	228,000
14	Tokyo Haneda	224,000
15	New York La Guardia	215,000
16	Frankfurt	207,000
17	Honolulu	198,400
18	Toronto	198,000
19	Washington National	193,500
20	Las Vegas	183,100

Major Airports of the World: Ranking by Cargo Handled, 1981

Ranking	Airport	Annual tonnage handled
1	New York JFK	1,191,500
2	Chicago O'Hare	792,500
3	Los Angeles	697,700
4	Frankfurt	600,000
5	Miami	573,300
6	London Heathrow	450,400
7	Paris CDG	447,300
8	Amsterdam	329,700
9	Atlanta	329,400
10	San Francisco	318,000

Traffic at United Kingdom Airports, 1981

Airport	No of passengers handled in 000s	Cargo tonnage handled
Aberdeen	1,545	8,000
Belfast	1,399	14,300
Birmingham	1,470	2,600
Blackpool	41	3,700
Bournemouth	140	8,000
Bristol	249	700
Cardiff	299	500
East Midlands	741	3,600
Edinburgh	1,120	900
Glasgow	2,267	12,400
Guernsey	495	7,700
Inverness	133	300
Isle of Man	292	200
Jersey	1,262	7,800
Kirkwall	77	500
Leeds/Bradford	351	300
Liverpool	279	9,300
London (Gatwick)	10,729	132,500
London (Heathrow)	26,400	450,400
London (Stansted)	261	6,600
Luton	1,973	13,400
Manchester	4,723	28,800
Newcastle	1,005	300
Norwich	135	300
Prestwick	361	17,800
Southampton	235	1,000
Southend	131	7,500
Stornoway	65	400
Sumburgh	531	3,300
Tees-side	244	200
Wick	34	100

Part Three

Abu Dhabi International UAE

Location: 7.5 miles SE of Abu Dhabi
Elevation: 13ft (4m)
Runways in use: 1
13/31 10,496ft × 150ft (3,200m × 45m)
Passengers handled in 1980: 1.6 million
NEW AIRPORT
Location: 19 miles from city
Runways in use: 1
13,400ft × 150ft (4,100m × 45m)
Passenger capacity: 3 million

Of the seven states forming the United Arab Emirates, the biggest and the official capital is Abu Dhabi.

The original airport was opened in August 1970 and, like some of its Middle Eastern contemporaries, is a beautiful creation, built by a British construction company. The terminal handled a total of over 800,000 passengers a year. The terminal complex consisted of three floors, accommodating departure and arrival lounges on a single level, with government and airline offices above. A VIP lounge and restaurant is on a third level. The control tower with air traffic services, meteorology and communications are housed in a structure incorporated into the terminal complex. Separately, there is a cargo building, a maintenance and overhaul building and a fire station, together with a large steel hangar. The whole airport is managed by the British firm of International Aeradio Limited under a contract with the Emirate of Abu Dhabi. The air traffic control services are performed by this well-known British company which also manufactured most of the ATC consoles in use in the tower. For long under British protection, the Gulf States now have an excellent commercial and operational association with British companies such as IAL, who

also provide training in airport management skills for Gulf airport personnel.

Completed in 1981, Abu Dhabi's new international airport has been designed to replace the original facility and provide a much more modern air terminal. The airport was delayed in its opening because of interior planning requirements, but is now understood to be fully operational, and its terminal has a capacity for three million passengers a year.

A new airport for Abu Dhabi was necessary particularly because of the noise problem for the city, and straightforward expansion of the other facility was not fully practical because of soil stabilisation problems. The new airport provides an elegant successor to the old, the design of which was the work of the Aéroport de Paris consultancy group.

The new airport has a very long runway, 4,100m long, with 18km of taxiways. The terminal has 11 aircraft positions, and there are another eight remote parking positions. A hydrant fuelling system has been installed.

The passenger terminal is in typically attractive arab style, and this and its cirular-shaped satellite building were built by two Japanese companies. After stepping off the passenger air bridge, an arriving passenger enters a large circular hall in the satellite building, in the centre of which is a column which mushrooms upward and outward until it blends into the roof, and in effect becomes the roof. The passenger then takes a moving walkway to the main building. Departure is on the same level in the other half of the building.

The attractive lines of arab sculpture were followed for Abu Dhabi's earlier Bateen airport, and which has now been joined by a new airport.

Amsterdam (Schiphol)

Netherlands

Location: 6 miles SW of Amsterdam
Elevation: 13ft (4m) *below* sea level
Runways in use: 4
09/27 11,325ft×200ft (3,453m×60m)
06/24 10,824ft×200ft (3,244m×60m)
01L/19R 10,640ft×200ft (3,300m×60m)
01R/19L, 11,150ft×200ft (3,400m×60m)
Airport area: 4,325 acres
Passengers handled in 1981: 9,669,000
Total air transport movements: 138,000
Cargo handled in 1981: 329,000 tonnes

There has been talk for some time in the Netherlands about the idea of creating a second major airport for Holland, but the Schiphol Airport Authority has no doubts that the principal airport now operating can cope with all traffic currently projected for up to, and probably beyond, the year 2000. If this proves so, Schiphol Airport will have been serving international air transport for the best part of 100 years.

Amsterdam's international airport lies on what was once the Haarlem Lake, which 400 years ago was a battle area for ships of the Prince of Orange and the Spanish fleet. The Haarlem Lake was drained in 1852, and the largest land reclamation operation then performed in the Netherlands was carried out. The task took five years. A stronghold was erected in the north-east corner and given the old name of Schiphol, which literally meant 'ships hole', or the grave of ships. In 1917 a military aerodrome was laid out at the foot of this strongpoint and also took the name Schiphol. Then, three years later, the Dutch

airline KLM began services from the airfield, and the site's life as a civil airport had begun.

As KLM developed, the airport became marked as the international airport for Amsterdam, and because it was so favourably located and in an area of completely flat terrain (Schiphol Airport is actually 13ft below sea level) it was ideal for its purpose.

Schiphol's site was also ideal for future development, and this development has been taking place progressively since 1926. In 1938 Schiphol became the second airport after Bromma (Stockholm) to have a system of paved, hard surfaced runways, and that year its original 190 acres were expanded to 520 acres. Today, the airport cover 4,325 acres, and is a Dutch showcase for international air traffic. In 1967 a completely new terminal complex was opened on what is now called Schiphol Centrum, and to the north-west of the previous facilities. Apart from providing a completely modernised terminal area for airport users, and which area offered a massive cargo warehouse, administration block, hotels and airline blocks, the developed central area also gave full scope to the tangential runway scheme, which provided for four runways disposed around the terminal facilities.

With the new terminal scheme, three piers were

One of the most popular and busy airports in Europe, Amsterdam's Schiphol remains under steady development, but is expected to serve Amsterdam and Holland well into the next century.

The horticultural scene is ever-present in Holland, as might be expected, and the main passenger terminal area at Schiphol Airport is relieved by numerous plant displays.

built, with a north and south pier on either side of a central pier, Pier B. The central pier was bifurcated at its extremity. All three piers had initial provision for 25 aircraft parking places. The first straight section of the central pier was equipped with a moving walkway for passengers. Holding lounges for departing passengers were arranged in the piers near each aircraft position.

In 1971, in order to provide for the wide-bodied jets and the traffic they were bringing, the southerly pier, Pier A, was extended with a short 'head' at its extremity, bifurcated in similar manner to the central pier. This added nine aircraft parking positions to raise the capacity of the terminal complex to approximately eight million passengers a year.

In order to provide further capacity, the terminal buildings were enlarged by 120% and as a feature of this extra work a completely new pier, Pier D, was constructed to the north, especially for wide-bodied aircraft, and further raising the capacity of the airport to 18 million passengers a year. The number of aircraft parking positions at the four piers A, B, C, and D was increased to 42. These extensions were introduced into service in April 1975, at which date 56 airlines were using the airport.

In 1974 work on the construction of a railway connection between Schiphol and the city of Amsterdam was begun and was opened in 1978. It was connected to The Hague and Rotterdam in June 1981. These rail services provide additional services for the passenger to the airport buses, operated by KLM and which connect with Amsterdam railway station.

Schiphol Airport is now one of the busiest airports in Europe handling almost 10 million passengers a year, and is one of the most attractive. It also has many interesting features, Not the least of which is its history and location, and which include the airport's own national aviation museum, and probably the biggest (and possibly also the duty-free shopping centre in Europe. The airport is also fourth busiest in Europe in terms of annual freight tonnage handled.

Anchorage International   Alaska

Location: 4.3 miles SW of city
Elevation: 124ft (38m)
Runways in use: 3
06L/24R 2,600ft×200ft (3,230m×61m)
06R/24L 10,897ft×150ft (3,320m×45m)
13/31 4,742ft×150ft (1,445m×45m)
Airport area: 3,995 acres
Passengers handled in 1978: 3,249,400
Total aircraft movements in 1978: 60,000
Cargo handled in 1978: 141,000 tonnes

Anchorage International Airport is run by the Alaska Department of Transportation and Public Facilities and is the main airport in the great State of Alaska. The airport is situated on a peninsula south-west of the city, and there are high mountains to the east.

Alaska International is a busy airport, and visitors are struck by the apparently never-ending stream of aeroplanes taking off and circuiting. After a few moments it will be observed that a large proportion of these aircraft are general aviation aeroplanes, for Alaska is a place of great distances, and large numbers of people in the State operate their own aeroplanes as a matter of course. There are, nevertheless, a good number of passengers handled by the commercial aircraft, especially in the summer season when the city has large numbers of visitors, for Alaska is increasingly a tourist destination, and

Anchorage International is the crossroads on one of the important air routes of the world today — the Polar Route.

has much to offer visitors, including remarkable scenic beauty.

Movements at the international airport and

26

general aviation facility are handled by separate controllers operating from the same control tower. On the airline front, Anchorage International is served by over 22 airlines, and has a two-level passenger terminal with adjoining international and domestic buildings with a pier and stands for some 20 aircraft. The airport is classified for Category II ILS operations.

General aviation operations include many seaplane movements, for there are many seaplanes based at the airport's general aviation centre, and a special seaplane area, consisting of two lakes, is designated for their use. The seaplane area has four designated alighting areas. For land-based general aviation aircraft there is a gravel runway, 2,200ft long × 100ft wide.

Ankara (Esenboga) Turkey

Location: 17 miles NE of Ankara
Elevation: 3,108ft (949m)
Runways in use: 1
03/21 12,306ft×200ft (3,752m×60m)
Passengers handled in 1980: 709,060
Total aircraft movements in 1980: 13,536
Cargo handled in 1980: 9,563 tonnes

Domestic traffic forms the larger part of the traffic handled at Ankara's Esenboga, one explanation for which is that much of this is carried on by government officials. In terms of movements, Ankara Airport handles about half the number at Istanbul. The airport of Ankara was opened in 1955 and is typical of the design of this period, with a long

terminal building having a principal entry and departure gate, and incorporating a central structure surmounted by the airport control tower. The airport works well enough, however, and is open 24 hours a day. It is located 17 miles from the city of Ankara, has one runway, and an apron capacity for nine B707-types at one time.

Both Istanbul and Ankara see a fair amount of military aircraft movements as well as civil, and at Ankara these are amounting to some 15.000 military arrivals and departures annually.

Ankara's Esenboga Airport.

27

Athens (Hellenikon/Spata-Saggani)   Greece

HELLENIKON
Location: 8 miles from Athens city centre
Elevation: 89ft (27m)
Runways in use: 2
15/33 11,550ft×200ft (3,520m×60m)
03/21 5,940ft×200ft (1,810m×60m)
Passengers handled in 1979: 10, 120, 953
Total aircraft movements in 1979: 110,959
Cargo handled in 1979: 65,730

SPATA-SAGGANI
Location: 17 miles from Athens city centre
Runways: 2
13,120ft×150ft (4,000m×45m) parallel
Airport to be opened for traffic in 1988
Passenger capacity in 1980: approx 22 million

The sun has always figured prominently in Greek aviation, from the time of the legend of Daedalus and Icarus whose elation on flying on wings of feathers and wax led them to disaster. Icarus came to know the power of the sun, and several million tourists have felt its attraction over the years as they have flown into Greece's principal airport on pleasure bent.

The present airport at Hellenikon was built on the coast, just eight miles from the centre of Athens, in 1936, when the modest facilities erected then comprised a single runway, a few hundred feet in length and two small terminals.

Immediately after the war, in 1945, development work on new and better premises began, but a halt was called to further work in 1950 with the decision to review the future potential of the site. A feasibility study for further expansion was approved in 1958 as the new big jet aircraft were coming on the scene, and a new construction programme was put in hand with the decision to retain the present airport site. It was decided also to purchase extensive additional areas of land to the east and south, and 1962, with financial and technical assistance from the US Government, further development was made. The

complete eastern sector of land was taken up for the construction of a new international terminal, while the original buildings on the north-west were retained for exclusive use by national carrier Olympic Airways.

This is the arrangement to the present day, with the international terminal — designed by famous Finnish architect Saarinen — seeing an increasing number of international arrivals annually. This terminal, which was inaugurated in 1969, had become so busy by 1975 that enlargement was considered necessary. At that date it was handling 1,201,000 tourists alone every year. In 1976 Hellenikon handled well over six million passengers of all categories, this traffic representing 70% of the total air passenger traffic through Greece.

This growth in air traffic has made its mark, however, and by the beginning of the 1970s it was clear that Hellenikon's days were numbered if traffic was to go on increasing at the present rate. The urgency for a new airport was eased with the introduction of the first wide-bodied jets and then the cut-back in flights at the time of the fuel crisis, but the lovely country of Greece is a strong attraction for tourists and when air transport recovered its earlier buoyancy the pressure was on Athens' airport once again.

Passenger traffic at Athens has been growing at an average annual rate of 11% for the past 10 years, and because of the resulting congestion it was understood that the improvements made could be nothing more than stop-gap actions until the day when a new airport was built to take over. Hellenikon has two runways with a bearing strength of 45,000kg SIWL, or enough to take the heaviest jets, and expansion of the apron has made it sufficient to handle six Boeing 747s at once.

Athens' Hellenikon airport is an attractive setting and backdrop for Olympic Airways' fleet, but will be replaced by a new airport at the end of the decade.

Apart from its limitations in size, however, Hellenikon presented problems by its airport noise, and in the past few years this has become a major issue. Because of the pressure over noise pollution and a recognition of the nuisance this causes to residents to resort areas such as Glyfada and Vouliagmeni, the Greek Government rejected proposals to further extend the life of Hellenikon, and finally pronounced, that it must close. This is expected by 1988, and the Government has said that the old airport will then be demolished, in 1990.

A master plan for a new airport was drawn up by three parties, under contract to the Hellenic Civil Aviation Authority, namely the Aéroport de Paris, Flughafen Frankfurt AG, and a Greek planning concern ADK. With final approval for this plan the new airport will be built on a site at Spata, approximately 17 miles from the city of Athens. The whole project is expected to cost some three billion Drachma.

Four sites were studied for a replacement for Hellenikon, at Tanagra, Vari, Spata-Saggani, and Lavrion, and for a variety of reasons three were rejected in favour of Spata, even though that site is almost twice the distance from Athens compared to Hellenikon. If the Spata Airport is built according to

The international terminal for foreign airlines handles a growing number of visitors each year. Transfer of all traffic to Spata-Saggani is scheduled for 1988-89.

the present plan, a motorway will be built also, to give high-speed connection. The new airport will be two and a half times the size of Hellenikon and handle traffic up to the year 2000. The airport will have two 13.000ft long parallel runways, with 5,000ft separation between them, and simultaneous take-offs and landings will be practised as traffic dictates. The initial handling capability of Spata will be for 15 million passengers a year.

There will be three circular terminal areas at Spata, with four-triangular holding lounges spaced around these terminals. The terminal areas will be spaced in a straight line and flanked by the parallel runways. On the other side of the access road from Athens and leading to the terminal areas there will be a maintenance area, adjoined by workshops and parking ramps, and at this end of one runway there will be a cargo terminal and a general aviation facility. At the extreme end of the airport will be the fuel farm. Spata airport is now expected to be open by 1988.

Atlanta International (W. B. Hartsfield)   USA

Location: 9 miles south of the city
Elevation: 1,030ft (312m)
Runways in use: 4
9R/27L 9,000ft × 150ft (2,743m × 45m)
9L/27R 8,000ft × 150ft (2,438m × 45m)
(to be lengthened to 11,889ft or 3,624m)
8R/26L 10,000ft × 150ft (3,048m × 45m)
8L/26R 9,000ft × 150ft (2,743m × 45m)
Airport area: 3,750 acres
Passengers handled in 1981: 37,594,100
Air transport movements in 1981: 523,100
Cargo handled in 1981: 329,400 tonnes

Atlanta held its place as second busiest airport in the world in terms of total passengers handled in 1981, and also in terms of air transport movements, while it ranked ninth busiest in the world in terms of cargo

tonnage handled. The airport is indeed an impressive air transport hub, and growth is such that while the airport is capable of handling 40 million passengers now, plans are already in hand for development to handle 75 million passengers in the future and by the end of the century.

Fifty years ago the good citizens of Atlanta, Georgia pondered hard on the whole business of airline travel. What the city needed most they thought then was another railway terminal. In 1925 aviation did not have too much going for it, it seemed, but the city found itself with the offer of a five-year rent-free lease on an abandoned speedway track, and when a subsidised airmail route was offered by the US Department of Commerce — providing someone could operate it — William B. Hartsfield declared himself ready to do something about it. Atlanta thought perhaps aviation might offer something.

The Atlanta City Council decided to take up the lease on the abandoned speedway, and installed night lighting and two, short dirt runways. The one thing required then was aircraft operators. These came by 1926, and Florida Airways was soon carrying mail and passengers to Miami. Two hangars were built and by 1928 the Atlanta-New York route was pioneered by Pitcairn Aviation, a forerunner of today's Eastern Air Lines.

Atlanta's airfield was still a poor dirt patch, however, as Charles Lindbergh discovered on a triumphal 48-State tour with the *Spirit of St Louis*. His aircraft stuck in the mud, and Bill Hartsfield and others had red faces.

By 1929, however, air routes from Atlanta stretched to New Orleans, Chicago, Miami and New York, and although the airport's administrators were still not certain about aviation, development was on the way. The airfield lease was near its end, so the city bought the field (for $94,500) and launched a programme to make the airfield the finest in the south-east. To do so, the airport was equipped with four men and two horse-drawn wagons. The Depression was now in train, however, and plans for expansion seemed doomed. Interest in using the airfield was so great, however, that the airport authorities borrowed city roadmaking equipment and used convict labour, and the runways were extended and the taxiways graded and approaches cleared. By the mid-1930s Atlanta Airport held claim to have the second largest number of air routes operating to points in the USA.

The airport site also became the home of an aircraft manufacturer, with the establishment of Lockheed Aircraft, which increased the traffic further. The need for a proper passenger terminal was now paramount, and the money for that was provided by

American Airlines advancing 10 years' worth of rental fees, or $35,000. So little cash was left from this generous advance, however, that extra funds had to be raised to buy furniture for the terminal, and this was done through the simple expedient of sightseeing flights.

Hartsfield International is today a far cry from the struggling airport of those years, when even the city fathers were doubtful about the whole business. The single storey terminal was replaced in due course, and a 1961 terminal was designed to handle 4.5 million passengers. It was later expanded to accommodate 14 million passengers, and this terminal ultimately handled 32 million passengers (in 1979).

The original site had also been changed by this time, for the one-time speedway base had long ago exhausted its usefulness. The crying need for a massive new airport site was eventually met with the purchase of two, 10,000-acre parcels of land to the north and north-west of the original location, and while under 4,000 acres is currently utilised, it is felt that the land now owned should meet Atlanta's airport needs for well into the future.

Escalating passenger loads led to the call for a brand new terminal in the mid-1970s, and ground was broken for this in February 1977. Opened in September 1980, it is now the main terminal facility at the airport.

Notable features of this new terminal include its location between the runways, to reduce taxying time, and which also allows quicker take-offs and landings and thereby reduced fuel consumption; a markedly simple design, with a series of straight lines channelling people, aircraft and cars into a smooth flow; back-to-back terminals which double the space available to arriving and departing travellers without lengthening their walk, and a self-contained concourse where Atlanta's very high number of transiting passengers are readily handled. Another feature is the automated train system, which carries up to 65,000 passengers a day between terminals and baggage claim stations. This Westinghouse system features 17 electrically-powered vehicles each holding 65 passengers with luggage.

For the future, Atlanta International is going to have a fifth concourse, expansion of the international passengers wing, additional cars on the rapid transit system, and improved flexibility of the gates to handle different types of aircraft. Additionally, what is claimed to be the largest cargo complex in the world will be introduced at Atlanta. General Aviation is equally being encouraged, and provision is being made to accommodate GA operators. In the future, Atlanta International should be capable of handling up to 75 million passengers a year, on four parallel runways through five domestic concourses with 180 aircraft gates.

Claimed to have the largest passenger terminal complex in the world today, Atlanta's Hartsfield International was newly opened in 1981 following a massive 'face-lift' and expansion programme.

Auckland International (Mangere)   New Zealand

Location: 13.5 miles south of Aukland
Elevation: 23ft (7m)
Runways in use: 1
05/23 10,800ft × 150ft (3,295m × 45m)
Airport area: 1,300 acres
Passengers handled in 1979: 2,583,071
Cargo handled in 1979: 74,783 tonnes

As the largest city in New Zealand, Auckland might be expected to boast an imposing international airport, and in fact the traffic passing through Mangere has made this the busiest international airport in the country. The city's size aside, contributing factors towards the busyness of Auckland International include the activity of Air New Zealand, the country's flag carrier, which has both its head office and operational headquarters in Auckland. Thus, this is the originating and terminating point for ANZ's international flights.

In terms of air transport history Auckland International is a young airport, for work on the site was only begun in 1960 and the airport was opened for business in its first stage of development in November 1965. The actual official opening date was 29 January 1966. Prior to this civil air services had taken place from the original RNZAF airfield at Whenuapai, which became unsuitable for air transport operations on a large scale.

The preliminary construction work took almost three years, and this included the reclamation of 160 acres of Manukaua Harbour, into which part of the airport was built to avoid absorbing more farmland than necessary. In this reclamation task 6.2 million cubic yards of rock and volcanic scoria were transferred from an extinct volcano on nearby Pukitutu Island.

In the first two weeks after the official opening, 10,000 passengers passed through Mangere Airport on 145 international flights, which served as an augury of the activity in store of New Zealand's principal international airport, and this promise has

been fulfilled over the years since. By 1970 passenger traffic had reached over one million a year, and this was up to 1.3 million by 1972. In 1978 traffic was totalling almost two million passengers annually, with 76,000 movements a year, a far cry from the 250,000 passengers recorded in the first year of operation.

Development has been phased at Mangere, with 24 buildings constructed in the first years of service, among them Air New Zealand's engineering hangar, which was the largest structure at the airport. The first passenger terminal was constructed from the outset as a temporary facility, with an intended life in the passenger-handling role of some five years. The purpose-built passenger terminal is now in service, and this unlovely building features an associate pier structure stretching across the apron and serving passenger aircraft by way of airbridges. This terminal is located to the west of the earlier terminal, which has now become a cargo terminal.

Other buildings erected as part of the complete Auckland airport development scheme include the operations building, radio receiving and transmitting stations, meteorological building, fire station, catering building and electrical sub-stations. There is an adjoining fuel farm, airline office buildings and an adequate collection of car parks. The tallest structure at the airport is the 104ft control tower, which has a control room 86ft up.

A feature of the site at Mangere, from which the airport takes its local name, is nearby Mount Mangere, which resembles a reclining man. The word *Mangere* is Maori for 'lazy', and the spot is said to have been named after this languorous image.

Auckland's Mangere Airport is the principal airport for New Zealand, and the hub now for the recently-opened New Zealand-London air services by flag-carrier ANZ.

Bahrain International (Muharraq)   Bahrain

Location: 3.5 miles from Manama City
Elevation: 5ft (1.5m)
Runways in use: 1
12/30 12,520ft×200ft (3,816m×60m)
Passengers handled in 1980: 2,900,000
Total aircraft movements in 1980: 36,500
Cargo handled in 1980: 27,000 tonnes

Bahrain earned a new place in the air transport history books when on 21 January 1976 it became the terminating point for British Airways' first supersonic Concorde service from London. When Britain and France began Concorde services on that historic day, in easterly and westerly directions, British Airways chose Bahrain as a stopping place on the long route to Singapore and Australia — the airline's ultimate objective.

The island State of Bahrain has, however, been a very important place in air transport for almost 40 years, for, in the days when Imperial Airways was forging air links to India and beyond, Bahrain was chosen by British Airways' original predecessor as the most suitable location in the Gulf for a major transit base, firstly for landplane and then flying-boat operations. From that time until just a decade ago, Britain's military presence was also strong, and the RAF force at Muharraq substantial.

Much of the former RAF camp is still used at the aerodrome, but today for civil aviation purposes, housing airline and administrative agency offices, which are all joined by an imposing international airport terminal.

It is through this terminal that pass the very many airline passengers travelling to and from Bahrain in an increasing tide, as the country's commercial importance grows, and which now make Bahrain International one of the newly important airports in

the world. As a Gulf State in its own right, Bahrain's prosperity is based on oil, which was first discovered in the country in 1932. Since the fuel crisis of 1973-74, however, this liquid gold has assumed new importance and the country's development bears witness to the prosperity the new demand is bringing.

The development of Bahrain International has gone hand-in-hand with this new interest, for in the last few years both passenger and cargo traffic have soared. This surge of traffic required an urgent expansion of the airport terminal, apron and operational facilities, and while much work has been done in this direction even more is required, and is being put in hand. When Concorde services began this increased the airport's importance further, and large sums of money were allocated by the Bahrain Government.

In terms of traffic, Bahrain's passenger throughput rocketed, from 274,526 passengers in 1972 to 1,650,000 in 1976. In 1977, it had gone up further to 1,880,000. Similarly, cargo traffic has soared, from the 5,000 tons handled in 1972 to the 27,000 tons moved through the airport in 1977. There was no less than a 52% increase in cargo tonnage handled in 1977 over 1976.

Because of this new movement, the British-built terminal building was given a new wing in 1976, and it was also provided with passenger loading bridges, to enable terminal-to-aircraft passenger loading to supersede the old procedure of passengers simply walking across the apron and up steps.

Bahrain Airport from the airside. Middle East crossroads airport, Bahrain is headquarters base for flag-carrier Gulf Air.

The terminal building now is expansive, airy and well-equipped with waiting facilities, restaurants and duty-free stores for passengers in their passage from the city to other places. Passenger flow requires departing travellers to pass through ticketing procedures on the ground floor, and thence up stairs to the departure lounge, from which exit is made by way of an airbridge to the cabin of the aircraft on the ramp. Outgoing baggage is processed through the building at ground level. Incoming passengers leave the aircraft cabin by the airbridges, and proceed from the arrivals hall of the building down stairs for baggage recovery. On the landside they take a taxi to the city. There is no airline bus service.

Some 23 international airlines operate to Bahrain, and to improve further the facilities at the airport both the Bahraini Government and a new agency, Bahrain Airport Services embarked upon a major investment programme, involving six million Bahraini Dinars (approximately £7.9 million). This money was to be spent on a purpose-built cargo terminal, an aircraft maintenance building, a new fuel farm, and a new inventory of ground support equipment. The

ground handling equipment will be bought steadily by the Bahrain Airport Services company, which was formed in July 1977 and granted the rights for all ground handling and ramp services at the airport by the Bahrain Government. The company took over this function from ASGUL (Airport Services Gulf), a subsidiary company of Gulf Air, which airline has its headquarters at Bahrain. BAS is a private company, with no government involvement, and which apart from performing ramp handling, operates the cargo warehouse, the airport restaurant and the flight kitchen — which produces no fewer than 12,000 airline meals a day. In taking over the work of ASGUL, BAS inherited a collection of various items of ground equipment, and plans to rationalise and modernise this equipment holding gradually. It is interesting to know that Concorde required no special equipment at all when it began its services, which in 1978 operated at a frequency of three a week from London up to the time of discontinuance of the service, in October 1980, when the through service to Singapore was terminated. A master Plan is in hand, for development of Bahrain to 1995.

Baltimore-Washington International   USA

Location: 10 miles south of Baltimore, 30 miles north of Washington DC
Elevation: 144ft (44m)
Runways in use: 4
10/28 9,450ft×200ft (2,880m×60m)
15R/33L 9,500ft×150ft (2,895m×45m)
4/22 6,000ft×150ft (1,828m×45m)
15L/33R 3,010ft×75ft (917m×23m) (general aviation)
Airport area: 3,200 acres
Passengers handled in 1979: 3,669,000
Total aircraft movements in 1979: 117,000
Cargo handled in 1979: 61,000 tons

Aviation began in Baltimore, Maryland, as long ago as 1784, when according to the records of the Maryland State Aviation Administration, a 13-year-old boy named Edward Warren lifted into the air on 24 June of that year in a balloon owned by a local attorney. The historic event is said to have occurred at Mount Vernon Place, about 12 miles north of where Baltimore-Washington Airport stands today.

The first airport for Baltimore was actually opened in September 1921. A municipal airport for the city was planned, but because of the Depression this did not actually open until 1941, by which time aircraft were already bigger and faster, and an even better airport was thus thought desirable. A master plan for this airport was submitted in May 1946 and construction of this began on a 3,200-acre site 10 miles south of Baltimore and 30 miles north of Washington DC. This airport was opened on 24 June 1950 by President Harry S. Truman and was officially named Friendship International Airport.

Since that time, Friendship International has become famous in American air transport circles because of the facilities provided to meet the first demands of the jet age, and which enabled record-

breaking flights to be made by the first Boeing 707s. Situated in the centre of an area with a population of more than five million, Friendship International was the only jet airport for the Baltimore-Washington region until 1962. By the early 1970s it was clear that the finance for extensive capital improvements being required should be provided by the State of Maryland and on 26 July 1972, therefore, the State of Maryland purchased the airport from the city of Baltimore for $36 million.

Following this, the role of the airport was reappraised, and it was decided that a prime objective was to develop the airport for the future to serve effectively the residents of all areas of Maryland as well as the Federal Capitol of Washington and surrounding states. To reflect this role the airport was renamed Baltimore-Washington International on 16 November 1973. At the same time a far-reaching expansion and modernisation programme for the airport's passenger terminal was put in hand, at a cost of approximately $65 million.

Under the plan the new terminal is 75% larger than the earlier facility. The architectural concept for the structure's exterior revolves around glass and steel, to give an airy and spacious feeling and admit plenty of light, the planner's intention being to eliminate the sight of any buff-coloured brick in the structure.

The expanded passenger terminal is capable of handling over 11 million passengers annually. Construction work began in October 1974 and was completed in 1980. The glass walls allow approaching passengers to identify readily the location of airline ticket counters, and 10 new entrances give direct access to these new airline ticket counter locations, which are so positioned as to decrease passenger walking distances by 60%. Aircraft gate positions are increased in number, and

33

all gates equipped with passenger holding lounges. In addition, each airline using the airport has its own separate baggage claim location on the lower level of the terminal, a feature which would undoubtedly be welcomed at other airports as a means of dramatically reducing the time spent by passengers waiting for baggage, time which in many areas of the world is becoming intolerable.

The new international arrivals wing incorporates passenger holding rooms for international and charter flights as well as a tax-free shop. There are enlarged Customs, public health and immigration

Baltimore-Washington has been an active airport serving the Federal Capitol and environs since 1950, and has undergone recent development to handle 11 million passengers a year.

facilities. Aircraft gate positions have been increased to 27 in number and boarding gates are equipped with passenger loading bridges. In addition, two mobile lounges, are used to carry travellers to their parked aircraft.

Belgrade International

Yugoslavia

Location: 12.5 miles from Belgrade
Elevation: 331ft (101m)
Runways in use: 1
12/30 9,842ft×197ft (3,000m×60m)
Passengers handled in 1981: 2,632,200
Total air transport movements in 1981: 36,200
Cargo handled in 1981: 22,300 tonnes

Belgrade international Airport was officially opened by the late President Tito in April 1962. Prior to this, the city of Belgrade was served from the early 1930s by an original airport, which had outlived its usefulness by the late 1950s.

Belgrade International is now a familiar airport to European travellers in particular, for whom a new international building was erected some five years ago. The airport is the main base for the national carrier, JAT, and also the prime terminal for some 25 international airlines which now serve Belgrade. The original two-level terminal, on the south side of the airport, has two concrete aprons with some 20 aircraft stands.

The airport is the subject of a moderate development programme, under which further expansion and improvement work is being progressively carried on.

Berlin (Tegel)

West Germany

Location: 5 miles from city centre
Elevation: 121ft (39m)
Runways in use: 2
08R/26L 7,990ft×200ft (2,421m×61m)
08L/26R 9,970ft×150ft (3,021m×45m)
Airport area: 1,137 acres
Passengers handled in 1981: 4,415,000
Air transport movements in 1981: 52,800
Cargo handled in 1981: 10,600 tonnes

West Berlin occupies the curiously unique place in the Federal German Republic of being located within East Germany's German Democratic Republic, and the three airports of Gatow, Tempelhof and Tegel, play a most important role in the transportation system connecting the city with West Germany. Gatow is operated by the Royal Air Force, while Tempelhof is generally closed to air transport movements, and Tegel thus remains the main hub of international air traffic for commercial passengers.

Operated by Berliner Flughafen-Gesellschaft (BFG), Tegel took over from Tempelhof as the main civil airport in 1975, when the size-limited airport of the old German capital was closed to commercial traffic, and Tegal is now served by some six international airlines, including British Airways, who operate scheduled flights with BAC One-Elevens.

Tegel is located to the north of West Berlin and slightly further away than the famous Tempelhof, which was right in the heart of the city. While advanced for its time Tempelhof's facilities would be no match today for the modern facilities of Tegel, which include radial terminals, the first of which is equipped with 14 passenger air bridge positions whose articulated structures extend across the apron. Provision for a second of these large, six-sided structures is made in the existing lay-out, and it is to be built as the traffic requires.

This terminal arrangement is a favoured style in the Federal Republic, the main terminals being flanked on the landside by an arrivals bowl and approach roads, which in turn are flanked by large carparks. The central bowl provides the entry point to the terminal building proper and through which passengers pass on their way to a flight. The main

Berlin Tegel Airport took over from Tempelhof to serve West Berlin's main commercial traffic, and is now the main civil airport linking the city to the Federal German Republic.

terminal is overlooked by the adjoining control tower and air operations building. There are two sets of roads leading to the terminal, on an upper and lower level, the upper for departing passengers and the lower level for arriving travellers. By way of these, buses, taxis and private cars reach the airport.

Berlin Tegel is playing an increasingly important role in West Germany's airline operations, and there is no doubt that the second six-sided terminal structure will be required before long, although no date has been put upon the construction of this easterly terminal.

Bombay (Santa Cruz)   India

Location: 8 miles north-east of city
Elevation: 27ft (8m)
Runways in use: 2
09/27 11,455ft×150ft (3,940m×45m)
14/32 8,956ft×150ft (2,730m×45m)
Airport area: 2,471 acres
Passengers handled in 1980: 5,046,540
Cargo handled in 1980: 69,000 tonnes

Civil aviation in India owes its start to J. R. D. Tata
and the late Neville Vintcent, who together founded
the airline which became the great Air-India of today.
J. R. D. Tata, chairman of Air-India until 1978, made
the first commercial flight to the old airport of
Bombay from Karachi in 1932, in a de Havilland Puss
Moth. This airport was at Juhu, on the edge of the
beach and no more than a series of mud flats. The
airfield served as an operational field for Tata Air
Lines until 1942, when a new military airfield was
established about two miles inland at Santa Cruz,
and this remains the site of Bombay International
Airport today. By the time Juhu was abandoned for
airline operations, concrete runways had been laid
down, but the site was inadequate for heavier airline
aircraft and could not be developed any further.

Santa Cruz became the main base for air transport
operations in Bombay, and has undergone much
development work over the years, with a number of
expansion programmes which made it possible to
handle first the Boeing 707s of Air India, and then
the Boeing 747s the airline now uses.

While his partner, Vintcent, had been killed in
World War 2, J. R. D Tata watched all this
development for 46 years until retiring from Air-
India. By that time, another development plan had
been put into train, covering a new international
terminal with three adjoining modules to form a
continuous shallow curve. The plan provided for
arrivals and departures to be handled on the first
floor of this building by way of 12 traffic piers.

The government appointed the Aéroport de Paris
as consultants to the new development plan, while
an Indian counterpart team was appointed with
members drawn from the Department of Civil
Aviation, the two national airlines (Air-India and
Indian Airlines) and members of the Indian Airport
Authority. The project was sanctioned in March
1976 and construction at the site began in 1977
with work on the terminal building proper
commencing in November 1977.

The terminal building was completed in 1980,
with work having to be shelved during the three
monsoons that intervened over the period — each of
which lasted for three months. There were
considerable delays due to shortages of steel,
aluminium and other materials, which delayed the
eventual opening of the terminal until February
1981. This terminal and its associate facilities are
now fully operational and handling a fast-growing
traffic.

Work covered the first of three modules of the
terminal, its associated apron, a remote parking
apron for eight aircraft, taxi tracks and a new cargo
terminal building. Of these items, the cargo terminal
was the first to be completed in April 1978.
Following installation of equipment, this terminal
began service in December 1980.

The new passenger terminal is a large, elegant
structure running in a long sweeping curve around
the aircraft apron and backed by sizeable car parks.
There is provision on the apron, immediately
adjoining the passenger terminal, for some 15
aircraft and there are now provisions for a further 12
aircraft on remote stands. The first module in the
terminal has a total floor area of 41,800sq m and a

*Bombay's Santa Cruz Airport was given a new
passenger terminal complex in 1981 as a feature of
the overall modernisation plan.*

capacity for 2.5 million passengers annually, with a peak hour throughput of 2,100 passengers.

Passenger embarkation and disembarkation is at mezzanine floor level, with arriving passengers proceeding from the mezzanine floor to the ground level concourse. Departing passengers enter the terminal at first floor level via an inclined ramp way, and after completing all formalities, move down to the mezzanine to await the call for boarding.

Inauguration of the first module of the international terminal was matched by the simultaneous laying of the foundation stone for an identical second module. This is scheduled to be completed about 1984, its purpose being to provide yet more capacity. There will be nose-in parking facilities for another four aircraft plus four remote parking stands. This module will be used exclusively

A 180m long ramp takes departing passengers to first floor of the Bombay Airport terminal, for check in and embarkation.

by Air-India and the airlines it handles. When fully developed, the terminal will have a total floor area of 120,000sq m and will handle up to 7.5 million passengers a year. By this stage, one module will be used exclusively for arrivals and the other for departures of foreign carriers, with the central module serving carriers handled by Air-India. The approach road for vehicles will then be doubled in width to serve all three modules, while a second exit ramp will be built adjacent to the third module. The car park space enclosed by the ramps will thus be doubled.

It is estimated that well before the end of the century the two runways will have reached saturation point, and the belief then is that it will be necessary to move to a fresh site, with a brand new airport for Bombay. For the moment, however, Bombay has a brand new airport terminal facility and, fittingly, J. R. D. Tata's old Leopard Moth hangs suspended from the roof in the large and spacious arrivals hall.

Boston (Logan International)   USA

Location: 1.5 miles from city
Elevation: 20ft (6m)
Runways in use: 5
04R/22L 8,800ft×150ft (2,667m×45m)
04L/22R 7,032ft×150ft (2,131m×45m)
15L/33R 2,468ft×150ft (748m×45m)
15R/33L 10,080ft×150ft× (3,055m×45m)
9/27 7,000ft×150ft (2,121m×45m)
Airport area: 2,400 acres
Passengers handled in 1981: 14,827,500
Air transport movements in 1981: 251,600
Cargo handled in 1981: 176,200 tonnes

Currently ranking as 15th busiest international airport in the world and 10th busiest in the USA, Boston's Logan International reaches its 60th anniversary year in 1983. In 1890 the land now occupied by the airport was completely under water, except for a few islands and a spit of land jutting into Boston Harbour from East Boston. Less than 35 years later, on 8 September 1923, Boston Airport was officially opened. Built on landfill dredged from Boston harbour, the airport then consisted of 189 acres, providing two cinder runways each 1,500ft long.

Today, Logan International Airport occupies 2,400 acres, with airside facilities that include five runways, one of which is over 10,000ft long.

Constituting what is known today as Massport, which is the ports and harbour undertaking operated by the Massachusetts Port Authority, Logan International has had a prominent role in air transport over the years, and since the early days of aviation when mail and passenger services began to develop. In 1927 the first regularly scheduled passenger flights opened between Boston and New York, a route that today is among the busiest in the United States. The strong growth of air transport really established Logan, and by 1948 it had grown to almost its present day size.

Massport, has operated Logan since 1959, and under its operation of the airport numerous development programmes have been planned and instituted, one of which was a $400 million programme completed in 1976, which saw

Boston's Logan Airport is largely surrounded by water although this picture does not give that impression. The Volpe International terminal is at foreground.

38

construction of the Volpe International Terminal, the south, south-west and north terminals, new parking facilities, and a 22-storey control tower, which is today the most prominent of the airport's landmarks. The airport is located in the core of the Boston urban area and is just three miles from 'down town' Boston. The airport occupies virtually all of a peninsula of land in Boston's inner harbour, and which is surrounded by part of East Boston, Winthrop, Revere and Chelsea. A vacant lot on part of the airport peninsula, known as Bird Island Flats, has recently been offered to interested parties for commercial development.

The airport's configuration is similar to that in other parts of the world (notably Tokyo's Haneda), where a complete island or peninsula of land is occupied by the airport, and this arrangement is valuable in some ways in that it gives the airport a certain integrity, without encroachment from adjoining land, be it industrial or agricultural. But this arrangement can also be inhibiting, for both terminal and runway enlargement. At Logan, however, development of the terminal facilities is still able to keep pace with traffic requirements, while should it be necessary to extend the runways any further, this could be done by building additional sections into Boston Harbour, although there could be some ultimate limitation there.

'Downtown' Boston is seen across the water in this aerial view of busy Logan International.

The airport is now an important employment centre for Boston, with some 12,000 people working there, with an annual payroll of over $200 million, while it is also a profit-earner for Massport, accounting for 70 cents out of every dollar earned by the authority. Airport revenues in 1981 were $72 million, and net operating revenues earned by the airport totalled $38 million for the same year.

With some 400 international flights every week now from Boston to Europe and the Caribbean, the airport is a most important traffic hub. Apart from the international services there are some 700 domestic flights every day, together with many general aviation movements. With some 200,000 tons of cargo handled annually, Logan's commercial importance is self-evident.

Terminal disposition at Logan stems from a central parking garage, with piers and box-like terminal structures ranging from this. The overall effect is to give the airport a low profile, the one tall structure at the airport being the new control tower building.

Brussels National (Zaventem)   Belgium

Location: 7.5 miles NE of Brussels
Elevation: 80ft (55m)
Runways in use: 4
02/20 9,247ft × 165ft (2,819m × 50m)
08R/26L 10,530ft × 150ft (3,211m × 45m)
08L/26R 11,930ft × 150ft (3,638m × 45m)
12/30 8,213ft × 150ft (2,504m × 45m)
Airport area: 2,717 acres
Passengers handled in 1981: 5,060,600
Total air transport movements in 1981: 81,700
Cargo handled in 1981: 156,000 tonnes

The capital city of Belgium has become of greater importance to European nations in recent years as the administrative heart of the European Economic Community, and much of the new air traffic generated by EEC comings and goings has benefited Brussels National.

The airport is the international air gateway for Belgium and was developed from the former military airfield of Zaventem in 1945. By 1956 the growth of air traffic called for a fresh development scheme, and a fine new terminal was planned. This new terminal, which incorporated the airport control tower, opened in 1961 but was largely destroyed by fire in early 1962. A reconstruction job was put in hand, however, and passenger handling was carried on in temporary facilities until the building was freshly opened.

The airport today is an attractive one for the traveller, offering comfortable passenger halls and waiting areas and with the desirable features of good restaurants and an excellent duty free shop. In 1973

The main terminal building at Brussels Airport (right-centre) was largely destroyed by fire in 1962 but rebuilt, together with the satellite terminal in foreground.

the main terminal was augmented by a satellite terminal somewhat remote from the main building and reached by a passenger pier, which is equipped with moving walkways. This radial terminal serves the aircraft which park around it by the medium of telescopic airbridges.

Further terminal developments are planned for Brussels National, although airport development is constrained somewhat by land limitations. One passenger facility worth mentioning is the hotel located within the transit hall of the airport building. Brussels airport is thus among those relatively few world airports which have their own airport hotel, situated on the airport site.

A particularly important area of traffic at Brussels in the last few years has been that of cargo, and the Belgium Airports and Airways Agency, which operates Brussels National Airport, erected a large cargo warehouse in 1965, with a capacity of 120,000 tons/year. Cargo traffic at Brussels National reached 150,000 tons in 1970, whereafter expansion of the cargo warehouse and cargo handling facilities was undertaken. The national airline SABENA, which handles the largest proportion of air cargo passing through the airport, also introduced its own cargo handling facilities, and a further dramatic development on the freighting front was made with the introduction in 1980 of a brand new Air Cargo Centre, called 'Brucargo'. This centre covers almost 250 acres, and cost the Belgian airport authority some BFr2.5 billion. It will allow steady increases in the cargo tonnage handled up to one million tons/year by the year 2000. The new cargo centre has been built immediately adjoining one of Europe's largest motorway interchanges, and therefore offers direct access to the routes to Antwerp, Liege and Ostend for the forwarders trucking cargo for air clients.

Buenos Aires (Ezeiza)

Argentina

Location: 12 miles SSW of city
Elevation: 66ft (20m)
Runways in use: 3
05/23 7,214ft×230ft (2,200m×70m)
11/29 10,827ft×60ft (3,300m×80m)
17/35 9,200ft×230ft (2,805m×70m)
Passengers handled in 1978: 1,472, 194
Total aircraft movements in 1978: 30,404
Cargo handled in 1978: 50,370 tonnes

Ezeiza is the principal commercial airport for Argentina and the capital city's main airport; there is another, smaller airport to the north-east of the city.

Ezeiza was planned in the 1940s as the major airport to serve Buenos Aires and the design originally had a tangential runway system with three pairs of parallel runways and a central terminal area. This plan was modified, however, and only three runways were eventually constructed. The design has been substantially modified further since 1949, when Ezeiza was opened by the Minister for Airports of the time, and the most recent development was completed in 1978, with a terminal modernisation programme designed to allow the handling of four million passengers annually.

This programme saw the construction of a new main terminal, with provision for some 11 aircraft served by passenger air bridges. This main terminal is flanked by one designed for specific use by the national carrier, Aerolineas Argentinas. In the development plan substantial underground parking space was provided and a hotel constructed also in the airport grounds and within a few minutes' reach of the passenger terminal. A usual range of restaurants, shops and duty free counters were incorporated together with banks and shopping areas.

Designed as a wedge-shaped structure, the passenger terminal is backed by a large park for cars and buses, in the familiar way on the landside. Auto-routes run from the centre of the airport, linking the terminal, to the city and outlying regions, to the north and north-west.

Cairo International

Egypt

Location: 12 miles ENE of city
Elevation: 381ft (116m)
Runways in use: 3
05L/23R 10,827ft×197ft (3,300m×60m)
05R/23L 13,120ft×150ft (4,000m×45m)
16/34 10,335ft×197ft (3,150m×60m)
Airport area: 2,965 acres
Passengers handled in 1977: 3,487,950
Total aircraft movements in 1977: 52,950
Cargo handled in 1977: 38,074 tonnes

Cairo is an historic stopping place on the world's air routes, for when Imperial Airways began services to Egypt in 1927 the Cairo services were quick to develop. The RAF aerodrome at Heliopolis served as the first Cairo airport, but in 1932 a civil airport was opened at Almaza just beyond Heliopolis. Almaza airport continued in operation into the 1950s, and had three runways, like Heliopolis before it. Almaza was in due course run down as a civil airport and is now a military aerodrome.

Then in World War 2 the United States Government built an aerodrome in the desert beyond Almaza, and this was known as Payne Field. This was later transferred to the Egyptian Government, and in 1946 it became the main Cairo airport and was named Farouk Airport.

Farouk Airport had three runways, and a terminal building on the east side of the airport. One of these runways, 05/23 was later extended to give a total length of 10,827ft (3,300m) and this remains the second longest runway of a parallel pair today.

In 1963 the terminal area was reshaped and relocated to the west, and a new terminal building was erected. This multi-storey structure was opened by President Nasser in May 1963.

A new instrument runway, 05R/23L, was brought into operation in July 1979 and this has a length of 4,000m. Further developments include a new terminal, and which was in construction at the time of writing. This new terminal should bring Cairo International Airport's capacity to 10 million passengers a year.

Cairo International Airport is an eye-catching terminal at an important location.

41

Chicago International (O'Hare)   USA

Location: 15 miles NW of Chicago
Elevation: 667ft (203m)
Runways in use: 7
14R/21L 11,600ft×200ft (3,536m×60m)
14L/32R 10,000ft×150ft (3,048m×45m)
9R/27L 10,140ft×150ft (3,090m×45m)
9L/27R 7,415ft×150ft (2,260m×45m)
4R/22L 8,070ft×150ft (2,460m×45m)
4L/22R 7,500ft×150ft (2,590m×45m)
18/36 (STOL) 5,341×150ft (1,628m×45m)
Airport area: 7,000 acres
Passengers handled in 1981: 37,976,400
Total aircraft movements in 1981: 554,500
Cargo handled in 1981: 792,000 tonnes

Over the years, Chicago O'Hare has retained its place as the busiest airport in the world, and continues to leave other airports standing in terms of both the number of passengers handled and air transport movements annually. As figures show, O'Hare is a very busy cargo airport also, and second only to Los Angeles International in tonnage handled amongst major airports. The sheer volume of activity is almost unbelievable in its immensity. In 1980 over 44 million passengers were handled on domestic, international, commuter, and other air carrier flights in a total of 639,919 aircraft movements. In 1980 over 800,000 tons of cargo were moved on domestic and international flights. Every day, 100,000 passengers (together with about the same number of visitors) pass through O'Hare Airport with the air passengers using the services of 42 major airlines, seven commuter operators, four supplemental carriers and a number of helicopter and other air carrier companies. There is an average of 1,900 aircraft arrivals and departures daily.

All of this development has occurred since the end of World War II, when Chigaco City Counil bought land and some facilities from the US Government as war surplus. What is now the site of Chicago's O'Hare Airport was originally known as Orchard Place, and which had been built during World War II by the Douglas Aircraft Company for the production of military transports. When the installation was declared surplus by the War Assets Administration, the city planners recognised that, because of its location and terrain, Orchard Place had the potential for development as a major airport for Chicago and to augment the existing Midway Airport, which was already under pressure. In January 1949, $2.5 million was authorised for new construction work, and the O'Hare Airport story had begun.

O'Hare opened its doors to domestic aviation traffic in October 1955. The name of Lt Commander Edward H. O'Hare, the United States' greatest naval hero, was conferred on the airport in December 1958, at which time international jet flights were beginning to make their impact, and the future role of O'Hare as an international terminal was recognised.

The first expansion programme at O'Hare was begun in 1959, and by 1961 traffic at the airport had

surpassed that at Midway to make O'Hare the busiest airport in the world. In 1963 the present terminal complex was dedicated in the presence of President John F. Kennedy. A new control tower almost 200ft high was built in 1971 and the runway system steadily enlarged from four to the present seven runways. Today, the whole complex of Chicago International covers 7,000 acres, and employs the services of over 28,000 people.

All scheduled passenger activity at O'Hare is concentrated in three main terminal buildings. International flights are handled in Terminal 1 while domestic flights are handled in Terminals 2 and 3. The buildings are linked together on the upper level enabling passage from one terminal to the next; there is also a free shuttle bus service for those who prefer to ride. The commuter airlines serving various midwest destinations operate from an ancillary terminal.

The sheer size of O'Hare makes it an impressive facility, with its Y-shaped pier structures on either side of a main terminal and vast parking lot on the landside capable of accommodating over 17,000 cars, some of them in what is the largest elevated parking structure of its kind in the world. For passengers there are numerous snack bars and cafeterias open 24 hours a day on the upper and lower levels of each terminal building, but in the Rotunda, a circular building located between Terminals 2 and 3, there are several restaurants and cocktail lounges on the upper and mezzanine levels. There is an O'Hare Hilton Hotel located directly opposte the main terminal complex, and this, of course, offers a further variety of restaurant facilities. The O'Hare Hilton has over 900 guest rooms, together with an arcade of shops on its lower level. It is reached by the pedestrian tunnels on the lower level of Terminal 2.

Other airport facilities include an inter-denominational chapel in Terminal 2; first aid stations, which include provision for nursing mothers; lost and found counters; airport information booths employing multi-lingual receptionists; 500 public telephones; US mail boxes in each terminal and two public observation decks which are open year-round from 8am to 9.30pm daily.

Other facilities at O'Hare include a main fire station with two satellite facilities, operated by the Chicago Fire Department, which allow fire fighters to reach any part of the field within three minutes. There is an air cargo area, comprising 13 separate cargo buildings, which house 27 airlines and six freight forwarders. The US Postal Service maintains its largest airport facility at O'Hare, and which handles 172,000 tons of mail yearly.

The seven runways at the airport include three sets of parallel runways and which range in length from 5,340ft to 11,600ft. The control tower oversees the operation of almost 640,000 aircraft movements each year. There are 27 operating positions in this tower, eight in the tower cab and 19 in the readar room. There are 125 air traffic controllers in the tower and 70 electronics technicians. ATC at the airport is the responsibility of the Federal Aviation Administration.

Chicago International is giving fresh attention to the task of handling future traffic and new consideration is being devoted to a plan for further use of Midway Airport. With the growing amount of traffic at Chicago's airports, an earlier plan provided for a new airport on an island site in Lake Michigan, but it is now felt that better use can be made of the existing airports, which include the third airport at Meigs Field. The City of Chicago Department of Aviation has spent some time preparing a detailed study for the new O'Hare, and this master plan was divided into three phases, with Phase 1 encompassing the initial development, Phase 2 including interim development and Phase 3 for development to the end of the century.

Chicago O'Hare retains its rank as the busiest airport in the world in terms of passengers handled and air transport movements annually.

The Phase 1 development was designed to cover work from the period 1982 to 1983. Phase 2 covers development from 1983 to 1987, and Phase 3 encompasses development from 1987 onwards. Under Phase 1, development was planned for terminals two and three, construction of an inter-terminal 'People Mover' system; construction of terminal four; construction of another concourse; construction of an apron area for this concourse, extension and relocation of the inner/outer taxiway system, and other related work. The improvements are intended to alleviate congestion and expedite passenger and aircraft movements. Additionally, they are intended to allow the airport facilities to better handle the latest generation of quieter, more economical aircraft, and provide a better level of service to air travellers.

No timescale has been put upon the construction and completion of this work, but it is expected that Phase 2 work will run on from the execution of the Phase 1 development.

Cologne-Bonn

West Germany

Location: 7 miles from Cologne and 15 miles from Bonn
Elevation: 295ft (90m)
Runways in use: 3
14L/32R 12,464ft × 200ft (3,800m × 60m)
14R/32L 6,120ft × 165ft (1,866m × 50m)
07/25 8,066ft × 150ft (2,459m × 45m)
Airport area: 2,470 acres
Passengers handled in 1980: 2,090,694
Total aircraft movements in 1980: 86,127
Cargo handled in 1980: 49,154 tonnes

The Federal German Republic must be given credit for establishing a system of airports which successfully serves all of the major cities in the country, and these airports have been brought to an advanced state, both constructionally and operationally, in the past few years.

Cologne-Bonn Airport is one of these modern airports, and is attractive both in its style and location, just seven miles from Cologne and 15 miles from the Federal capital of Bonn. The airport started life as an airfield for the Luftwaffe in 1938, at a location known as the Wahner Heide. It was enlarged somewhat by the occupying forces in the period 1945-50, and then first discussions about providing a civil airport to serve both Cologne and the newly designated Federal capital of Bonn were held in 1949. In 1950 approval was given for the development of the civil airport, and it was arranged that the principal shareholders in the operating company should be the German Federal Republic and Land of North Rhine-Westphalia, and the cities of Cologne and Bonn.

On 1 February 1951 the airport was transferred to

Cologne-Bonn is the principal airport serving the Federal German capital, and is notable for its distinctive star-shaped arrival/departure buildings.

The long-term plan for Cologne-Bonn Airport is the construction of four star terminals, attached to the main building.

German administration, and the unfolding story of growth to great strength commenced. When West Germany's own airline, Deutsche Lufthansa, began postwar operations in 1955, the airport began to play an increasingly important role.

A programme of development began in 1958 to bring the airport up to international standard, and in 1970 the inauguration of the new terminal, on 20 March, saw the completion of the work. Today, the interesting arrangement of the airport provides for drive-in facilities, where cars or buses may be taken straight to the terminal buildings on specially constructed roads, to deposit their passengers at concrete, steel and glass buildings for check-in.

This check-in is performed through a decentralised system, which abandoned the usual idea of a large central hall with rows of ticket counters in favour of a terminal building with two star-shaped satellite buildings each containing six check-in counters. Under the first section of the project, there are two satellites linked to the main horseshoe-shaped building, but with ultimate realisation of the plan there will be four in all, disposed around the main building. The main terminal itself has six floors and its wings have four. The departure level for passengers is on the first floor, and they exit from the satellites to the aircraft by way of airbridges. The check-in units are directly related to individual aircraft positions, thus only passengers for the same destination assemble together, and domestic and international flights are handled under the arrangement without conflict.

The satellites also admit arriving passengers, who make their way by the airbridges to the main building where they finally arrive at ground level by way of stairs and escalators, reclaiming their baggage in the process.

The present capacity of the airport is approximately 3.5 million passengers a year. When it has reached that capacity the two extra star terminals will be added. It is calculated that the airport will be perfectly capable of handling 206,000 aircraft movements a year in the year 2000.

Copenhagen (Kastrup)

Denmark

Location: 5 miles SSE of Copenhagen
Elevation: 17ft (5m)
Runways in use: 3
04L/22R 11,800ft × 150ft (3,600m × 45m)
04R/22L 10,825ft × 150ft (3,300m × 45m)
12/30 9,184ft × 150ft (2,800m × 45m)
Airport area: 2,583 acres
Passengers handled in 1981: 8,192,100
Total air transport movements: 134,300
Cargo handled in 1981: 139,600 tonnes

The big question mark hanging over Copenhagen Airport for the past few years has concerned the development of Saltholm. The island of Saltholm lies in the sound between Denmark and Sweden and has been uninhabited except by birds. It was decided in 1968 that Saltholm was the best possible site for an airport which could provide for growing traffic in Scandinavia and which could replace Kastrup. Kastrup had served Denmark well as its international gateway, but was size-limited.

When the remarkable growth in traffic of the 1960s and early 1970s slowed, a reappraisal was given to the Saltholm Airport project. While Saltholm offered much from the environmental standpoint, the cost of developing this site would clearly be astronomical, and it appeared that such an airport might not be needed after all — at least until the end of the century, by which time aircraft might be quite different in form and operational character.

The seal was set on the Saltholm idea in June 1978 with the report to the Copenhagen Airports Authority by the committee set up to investigate conclusively the scheme. The Copenhagen Airport Committee of 1975 ruled, with its report, that Saltholm project should not be proceeded with. In other words, the Saltholm island airport was 'dead' — at least for a good many years to come.

Aerial view of Copenhagen shows the limited prospects for expansion of the airport, but which is expected to serve Denmark for many years to come.

Kastrup, it was decided, should remain the international airport for Copenhagen, for a number of reasons. For one, it would be much cheaper to extend Kastrup than move to Stalholm. The rate of growth in traffic at Kastrup suggested that the present airport would still be able to cope with the passenger throughput up to the end of the century, and, moreover, the capacity of the main runway system would be sufficient for the amount of traffic expected up to the year 2000. For capacity purposes, in fact, there would be no need to alter the runway system. It would be possible to make extensions to the terminal buildings and aircraft handling stands within the existing airport boundaries.

Kastrup, then, will go on serving Denmark's capital city in the way it has done since it was opened over 50 years ago, on 20 April 1925. It has undergone many changes since that date, and will undoubtedly undergo more, but its familiar and friendly form will continue to greet passengers passing through, for this is the prime international hub for Scandinavian traffic. The three-nation air partnership representing Norway, Denmark and Sweden in the form of the national carrier Scandinavian Airlines System (SAS) regards Kastrup as its principal operational base, and, amongst other things, has its air cargo terminal at the airport.

From the 5,000 passengers that used Copenhagen Airport in 1925, traffic is now up to 8 million travellers annually. It is expected to be of the order of 22 million by the year 2000, when further changes will have been made to the terminals; the present international terminal can be extended eastwards as well as westwards.

Dallas-Fort Worth   USA

Location: 17 miles from both Dallas and Fort Worth, Texas
Elevation: 596ft (179m)
Runways in use: 3
17R/35L 11,400ft×200ft (3,474m×60m)
17L/35R 11,400ft×200ft (3,474m×60m)
13L/31R 9,000ft×200ft (2,743m×60m)
Airport area: 17,800 acres
Passengers handled in 1981: 23,533,900
Total air transport movements in 1981: 445,800
Cargo handled in 1981: 218,400 tons

One of the most remarkable airports that has been brought into being in the last five years in Dallas-Fort Worth, which typfies the American approach to building on a grand scale but which could well be one of the last really big airports to be constructed in the world. While the airport does not occupy all of the land allocated to its site, this site covers 17,800 acres; centres of population in most countries of the world no longer have such areas readily available for development.

While the airport is new in operational terms, its history is long and in fact goes back to 1927. In that year the city of Fort Worth, Texas, moved into commercial aviation with the construction of Meacham Field. Discussions were held with Dallas about the idea of a regional field to serve both ciities, but the talks came to nothing and Dallas then gained its own airport with the purchase of the US army airfield, Love Field, in 1928. In 1940 both cities asked the Civil Aeronautics Administration for help to expand their airports and again the question was raised of developing a combined regional facility, but again the talks dragged on and in the meanwhile both Love Field and Fort Worth airports were independently developed. In May 1961, however, the Federal Government indicated it would like to see the two cities cooperate on a single airport, and the Civil Aeronautics Board and FAA supported the concept of a regional airport. In 1965, after more months of discussion the Dallas-Fort Worth Regional Airport Board was organised, and that year the Texas Legislature approved the creation of an authority to govern a new airport. In April 1968 funding and the planning and construction of the new airport were authorised and ground-breaking ceremonies began in Decmeber 1968. Drainage work on the site began in January 1969 and five years later, to the month the airport opened for business.

Apart from its size, the notable thing about Dallas-Fort Worth is that it is built literally between the two cities, 17 miles from the central business districts of both, and serves the two Texas communities primarily. It is, of course, designed as an international airport, and in the few short years that it has been operational has demonstrated its importance to the American air transport business by becoming the fourth busiest airport in the USA in terms of air transport movements.

As the illustrations show, Dallas-Fort Worth is not only big but it is a good-looking airport embodying advanced ideas, and it is interesting to know that in arriving at the design the airport's planners made use of computer simulation studies to determine the airspace demands and then requirements for airport growth. From these came the concept of a multi-terminal facility served by a central, spine road, and flanked by long parallel runways for simultaneous take-offs and landings. The master plan for the airport was based on airspace demands for up to 178 aircraft movements an hour under instrument flight rules, or, in fact, near saturation conditions. To handle this number of aircraft, 11 runways were built into the master plan and as many as 13 terminals. In true Texas tradition, Dallas-Fort Worth was made big, and much bigger than is actually required at the present.

For the moment at least, the airport has four terminals and three runways, two of which are the north-south parallel runways, 11,400ft long and 200ft wide, and the third runway being a cross-wind runway of 9,000ft length. As with all of the runways planned, the present strips will handle aircraft weighing up to 400 tons and are fully equipped with instrument landing systems for Category II operations.

The terminals offer 75 boarding gates and are

used at the moment by six international airlines, 10 domestic carriers and seven commuter operators. The terminal structures are semi-circular in design and based on the 'drive-to-gate' concept, which means that a minimum amount of distance for walking is required of the traveller from the point where he parks his car, on the landside of the terminal, to the point where he boards his aeroplane. The concept is followed throughout the airport and the individual terminal areas are reached by the International Parkway spine road and which connects at either end with state highways, 183 on the south and State Highway 114 at the north.

For moving between various points on the airport there is an Airtrans system, and this electrically powered automatic transit system moves passengers and employees from terminal to terminal and to and from remote parking areas as required. The Airtrans system, made by the Vought Corporation, is a permanently operating 'people-moving' system which has a special place at big airports and which is seeing increasing use as a safe and efficient method of movement. Airtrans at Dallas-Fort Worth consists of 51 passenger vehicles,

Air travellers' complaints about long walking distances seem well illustrated here at Dallas-Fort Worth, an airport which has given special attention to this problem of air travel.

each of which carries up to 40 people. In the first three years of operation at DFW Airtrans carried 10 million riders.

In financial terms Dallas-Fort Worth Airport is already regarded as a good servant to its communities, and the activity at the airport generates more than $1.5 billion annually through the purchase of supplies, goods and services, and this in itself gives direct economic benefit to the many hundreds of businesses and thousands of individuals in the region. Some 43,000 people are now said to be earning all or part of their livelihood from Dallas-Fort Worth.

Airside view of Dallas-Fort Worth Airport shows one of the semicircular terminal areas, located along the International Parkway spine road.

Damascus International
Syria

Location: 14 miles SE of Damascus
Elevation: 2,020ft (616m)
Runways in use: 2
05R/23L 11,811ft×150ft (3,600m×45m)
05L/23R 8,860ft×150ft (2,700m×45m)
Passengers handled in 1977: 970,808
Total aircraft movements in 1977: 18,988
Cargo handled in 1977: 60,998 tons

The Syrians say, quite rightly, the Damascus is one of the most ancient cities in history, and this busy Middle-Eastern crossroads certainly has an atmosphere of the past which is strongly impressed upon the visitor. Situated at the eastern end of the Mediterranean, between Turkey, Jordan and Iraq, Syria is an important gateway to the Middle East, and its capital city deserving of a good international airport.

The new airport for Damascus was built over the period 1965-69 following a study made in 1955 which concluded that a new airport should be built to replace the original airport at Mezze. Mezze had been functioning for many years as the airport serving Damascus, but was quite unsuited for jet operations. The site for the new airport was determined by a German planning team, the Becker Institute, the final outcome of which was the location of the airport at the favoured site of Jdaidat El Khass, 14 miles from the city centre. While a good taxi ride from the city (the usual medium of transport for passengers) the site offered unimpeded take-off and landing prospects well away from hills, good drainage qualities of the soil, and excellent bearing characteristics of this soil for heavy aircraft. Now the prime international airport for Damascus, the airport at Jdaidat El Khass is situated ESE of the city between the towns of Rhassole and Jdaidat El Khass, and at an elevation of 2,020ft.

Unfortunately, construction of the beautiful terminal building had a chequered career, for while work began on this in 1970, its completion was deferred when costs escalated, and only in 1974 was further work done on bringing the design up to date. In July 1976 the Syrian Government awarded a contract for completion of the terminal to a Syrian firm, the General Company for Building of Damascus, to impress the terminal into service speedily. Meanwhile this fine passenger terminal had still to be completely finished and it was giving way to the adjoining freight terminal, which had been converted into the passenger building pending completion of the passenger terminal proper.

The new Damascus International Airport is an elegant and well laid-out facility designed for the processing of two million or more passengers a year. It has two runways, parking space for up to 16 big jets on the apron within walking distance of the terminals, and is an impressive aerial gateway to the Syrian Arab Republic. A slender, 138ft high control tower oversees the runways, which are equipped with Category II ILS. VOR and DME aids are available, together with VHF and Tropilog receivers.

Damascus Airport is the location for the air traffic control centre for the Damascus Flight Information Region, and which covers airspace extending over Syria, Jordan and the northern part of Saudi Arabia. The parallel runways offer up to 11,800ft length.

Damascus Airport control tower.

Delhi (Palam)
India

Location: 8 miles SW of city
Elevation: 744ft (227m)
Runways in use: 3
09/27 7,520ft×150ft (2,292m×45m)
10/28 12,500ft×150ft (3,810m×45m)
15/33 6,750ft×150ft (2,057m×45m)
Passengers handled in 1977: 2,571,414
Total aircraft movements in 1977: 53,672
Cargo handled in 1977: 37,000 tons

The International Airports Authority of India (IAAI) is responsible for Delhi Airport, as it is for the other main airports of India, at Bombay, Calcutta and Madras, and in recent times Delhi's Palam Airport has been the subject of a development and modernisation scheme as a feature of the overall improvement plan.

Air transport first came to Delhi in the early 1930s, following the creation of Tata Air Lines, which became the principal airline in India. India was then under the rule of the British Raj, and the Viceroy of India opened the new Willingdon Airport in February 1936. This airport was used up until the war, when aircraft up to DC-3 weight used it with growing intensity. Another airport was built to the west during the war, however, and this airport, at Palam, was in more open countryside and proved more suitable for large-scale development.

After World War 2 Palam Airport became the principal airport for Delhi, and was consequently given progressive attention, for development and enlargement until in 1972 the Aéroport de Paris consultancy organisation was given the task of producing a master plan for the Delhi Airport terminal area. Under this plan, a series of terminals would form a large circle, with the circle broken by a segment occupied by the approach road system.

This plan has undergone some change since then, but a new passenger terminal has been constructed incorporating international and domestic sections. Subsequent to that work a new international terminal has been scheduled for construction by 1984, and when this new facility is brought into service the earlier building will be used for domestic services alone. Domestic services will be transferred to a new domestic terminal to be erected by about 1988. Ultimately, Delhi airport is intended to be capable of handling 40 million passengers and 70,000 tons of cargo annually.

In 1982 work had been completed on an extension to the international arrival hall, and which will provide 40% additional space for passenger handling for the moment. Work has also been commenced on a new international cargo complex.

Denver (Stapleton International)   USA

Location: 7 miles from Denver
Elevation: 5,330ft (1,615m)
Runways in use: 4
35R/17L 12,000ft×200ft (3,636m×61m)
35L/17R 11,500ft×150ft (3,485m×45m)
8R/26L 10,000ft×150ft (3,030m×45m)
8L/26R 7,925ft×150ft (2,401m×45m)
(general aviation)
Airport area: 4,500 acres
Passengers handled in 1981: 22,601,900
Air transport movements in 1981: 379,300
Cargo handled in 1981: 135,900 tonnes

Denver's Stapleton International claims to be the seventh busiest air carrier airport in the USA in terms of passenger volume, and the fourth busiest in landings and take-offs. Owned and operated by the city and county of Denver, Colorado, as a division of the Department of Public Works, the airport is said to be the air transport hub of the Rocky Mountain region, and is a major connecting point for both trans-continental USA and north-south flights.

It was not always so, of course. Mayor Ben F. Stapleton paid $143,000 for a 630-acre cow pasture on the prairie in the 1920s, when it was derisively referred to as 'Stapleton's Folly'. The airport terminal is still located on the site of that cow pasture, with the surrounding airport now occupying 4,500 acres of prime real estate, and which is not referred to as a folly today. Denver Municipal airport was dedicated in October 1929 and has been steadily expanding ever since.

When the airport opened it consisted of four, unsurfaced runways, a two-storey terminal building, a hangar and a combination ambulance and fire station. The second floor of the terminal contained three rest rooms for pilots and a radio room. Over the

Denver, Colorado's Stapleton airport is one of the country's highly situated airports, built adjoining the Rockies. Some idea of the traffic is given by the picture, and which is now totalling 23 million passengers/year.

years, Stapleton International developed to take in other grazing land real estate. The old terminal buildings have been replaced by a purpose-built passenger handling complex coupled with air operations buildings. There is now more land under concrete than the entire airport occupied when it was originally built. However, about 900 acres is still given over to wheat and other crops on the airport land. Some 10,000 trees have been planted around the edge of the airport, and much of the area adjoining residential neighbourhoods has been landscaped with lawns and flower gardens.

The airport's terminal complex comprises a half-circular building from which three main piers extend across the apron in the direction of the four runways, which run north-south and east-west. The terminal complex is a three-level structure, the first of which, Grade level, is for baggage handling and related services. The second level is for passenger check-in and ticketing, and the third level, Mezzanine, houses airline offices and observation decks; this level also carries bridges which lead directly to elevated car parks on the airside. The ticketing level houses the gate rooms which lead directly to four concourses, with their piers to the aeroplanes. The four concourses, A, B, C and D, are served by specific airlines, of which there are some 25 in all, including commuter airlines.

Spread over the 4,500 acres constituting Stapleton International are various hangars, catering company offices, fire-stations, air cargo buildings, car parks, fuel facilities and car rental firms, together with the engineering and maintenance bays and sundry services which go to making up the busy

airport of today. Where Denver is concerned, these also include general aviation hangars, a heliport and a small US Army facility.

The city and county of Denver owns all the land and improvements on the airport, except a few small hangars and service buildings. The airport is entirely self-supporting and receives no revenues from the city. Numerous retail shops and service facilities contribute towards the airport's sizeable income, which today is such that over 12,000 people are employed at the airport with a combined payroll approaching $500 million annually.

In terms of traffic about 23 million passengers are now being handled at Stapleton International — which is an increase of over 300% in the decade. Passenger traffic is projected to reach 35 million by 1990, and for this reason the Department of Public Works is constantly looking at areas where development may be required to handle the traffic growth. Aircraft movements, now totalling some 500,000 a year, are now double those of 1955. Some three quarters of this total is attributable to scheduled air carriers, with general aviation and commuter airlines generating the remainder. During the skiing season, hundreds of charter and special flights converge on Denver, for the Rocky Mountains are a strong tourist attraction (there are 53 peaks above 13,000ft in the State of Colorado).

Stapleton International Airport currently has parking facilities for 72 aircraft, and the airport says it will accommodate everything from four-passenger Cessnas, to 500-passenger Boeing 747s. Direct airline service is available from Denver to every major city in the USA.

Detroit-Metropolitan (Wayne County)   USA

Location: 17 miles from city centre
Elevation: 639ft (195m)
Runways in use: 4
03L/21R 10,500ft×200ft (3,200m×60m)
03C/21C 8,500ft×200ft (2,591m×60m)
03R/21L 10,000ft×150ft (3,048m×45m)
09/27 8,702ft×200ft (2,562m×60m)
Airport area: 6,800 acres
Passengers handled in 1981: 8,816,300
Total aircraft movements in 1981: 158,700
Cargo handled in 1981: 83,500 tons

Detroit falls into Michigan's Wayne County, and the County Board of Commissioners decided to build an airport first in 1929 on a site approximately one mile square. This was known as Wayne County Airport, and services began on the field in April 1929. As air transport gathered momentum in the USA in the 1920s and early 1930s, Wayne County Airport was among the first to have a control tower.

In 1942 the airport was turned over to the US Army, and it was also joined during this period by another aerodrome, Willow Run, which was built specifically to serve a new aircraft factory; Ford Motor Company's famous plants in Detroit were turned over to war production, including the

manufacture of aircraft. Because of its better facilities, US scheduled airlines transferred their operations to the new field at Willow Run, and this situation continued until the end of World War 2 when Wayne County Airport was given a fresh lease of life with its handing back to the civil authorities and the allocation of money to develop the airport as a major international facility.

With this plan, the Wayne County Commissioners proceeded to treble the size of the airport, and US domestic airlines and then overseas carriers, such as BOAC and Pan American World Airways began using Wayne County from the mid-1950s. American Airlines and Allegheny Airlines (now US Air), and then Northwest Airlines began using the airport from 1958. A new terminal was opened to handle jet aircraft services from December 1958 and the 09/27 runway was extended to serve the needs of jet aircraft in 1965.

Because of increasing traffic, a second terminal was built in 1974, and this was called the Michael Berry International Terminal. Since then, further terminal development work has been carried out, and a 3,048m runway, 03R/21L, built. The runway complex is somewhat unusual at Detroit-Metropolitan, in that 03L/21R, and its fellow 03R/

21L, are separated by a third, central runway, 03C/ 21C. There was in fact a fifth runway, 15/33, at one time, but terminal development led to its olosure. Plans are in hand now for the construction of an entirely new terminal complex at Detroit-Metropolitan, the arrangement for this complex to be located south of the present terminals.

The one-time airport of Willow Run is still extant, and may be turned into an air cargo centre and general aviation airport for Wayne County.

Dubai International   UAE

Location: 3 miles east of Dubai city
Elevation; 24ft (7m)
Runways in use: 1
12/30 12,557ft×150ft (3,805m×45m)
Passengers handled in 1981: 3,156,762
Total aircraft movements in 1981: 59,161
Cargo handled in 1981: 62,069 tonnes

There are seven states in the United Arab Emirates; Dubai is one of them and has perhaps one of the best-looking airports in the region. It does not come entirely from new-found oil wealth, for the British firm of constructors Richard Costain Limited created this in 1971, to a contract valued at £4 million, but as with all airports in the Gulf and UAE much of the new-found affluence has been turned into the latest aids and equipment, to the benefit of users and operators alike.

Dubai is putting much into its economy to improve the standards of living of its citizens and an increasing number of visitors, and much effort is going into diversifying industrial and commercial development to make the region less dependent upon oil in the years ahead. It is a major objective, for example, to make the UAE self-sufficent in food, and for this reason agricultural procedures are being modernised. In Dubai itself a dry dock capable of accommodating super tankers is being built, and a satellite communications centre has been concentrated at Jebel Ali, near Dubai, to provide international telephone, telex, high-speed data and colour television transmission facilities. A Dubai trade centre has also been built.

All of this activity has been manifest to a large degree in passenger and cargo traffic increases through the airport, and some of the figures recording this situation are quite remarkable. It should be noted that the cost of air freight has been of relatively minor significance to those on the receiving end, and for this reason all kinds of commodities, products and materials have been airfreighted in. When the sea port at Port Rashid became congested with ships and airport took on even more work as shippers turned to the air.

The result of all of these factors has been to produce traffic figures which show increases of several hundred per cent. In 1972, for example, 6,880 tons of cargo were moved through Dubai Airport. In 1975 the loaded and unloaded total was 15,000 tons, and in 1981 this tonnage was now up to 62,000 annually. In terms of passenger traffic there have been similar dramatic increases.

The airport terminal facilities have been considerably enlarged and modernised in the last few years for the 34 scheduled and non-scheduled operators that use the airport, and the government recently allocated Dirham 800 million for further work. This work includes construction of a second runway and a new terminal. The present facilities are certainly capable of handling the current traffic, but the astonishing growth rates that have been experienced have led the authorities, wisely, to prepare for substantial future growth.

It is by no means certain that Dubai will see massive future traffic, however, for an abundance of airports has been built in the Gulf in recent times and more have been planned. Just 12 miles from Dubai is Sharjah Airport, and to the north at Ras Al Khaimah a new airport was opened in March 1976. Yet another airport near Dubai, at Jebel Ali, 17 miles to the south-west has been planned. The future plan provides for a new arrivals terminal, airbridges, additional car parking, and two apron control buildings.

The elegant lines of Dubai Airport are shown well in this night-time picture of the British-built terminal complex.

Dublin

Eire

Location: 5.5 miles north of city
Elevation: 221ft (67m)
Runways in use: 3
05/23 7,540ft×200ft (2,286m×61m)
17/35 6,841ft×200ft (2,073m×61m)
11/29 4,475ft×200ft (1,356m×61m)
Airport area: 1,500 acres
Passengers handled in 1981: 2,729,100
Air transport movements in 1981: 41,700
Cargo handled in 1981: 37,400tons

Planning and site selection for the present Dublin Airport began in 1936 when the site of a previous Royal Flying Corps base, at Collingstown, appeared the most favourable. This was some 10 miles from the nearest mountains, the approaches were obstacle free, and the weather conditions were excellent. Most importantly, the site was close to Dublin's city centre. In 1937 a new main grass runway had been laid and in 1940, after extensive work on the site, the first flight from the new civil airport took place.

In the spring of 1941 the new terminal building was ready for passengers. This had been designed by a 25-year old architect, Desmond Fitzgerald, and was impressive enough to earn him a gold medal from the Royal Hibernian Institute of Architects.

In the immediate postwar years the increases in traffic and aircraft size made a rigid runway system essential, and three new concrete runways were planned. The longest of these, some 5,000ft, was finished in 1947. By 1950 the number of passengers using the airport numbered some 150,000.

Throughout the 1950s Dublin Airport continued to expand, and existing aircraft hangars were enlarged a new ones built. By 1957 British European Airways, Sabena of Belgium and BKS of Britain were operating scheduled flights to the airport. In 1958 National carrier Aer Lingus began trans-Atlantic operations, and the terminal building required further expansion. In June 1959 a new North Terminal building was opened in the form of an arrivals area.

Runways and hangars were once again extended as jet aircraft began operating regularly in the 1960s. By 1969 the two main runways were long enough for the Jumbo jets, which were only a short while away. The main event of the 1970s was the opening in 1972 of a new passenger terminal complex to handle passengers from the Jumbos. Capable of handling some four million passengers a year, this terminal is now seeing a throughput of over 2.5 million passengers annually. The passenger terminal complex was also joined in the 1970s by a new cargo terminal, with a capacity for some 40,000 metric tonnes of freight.

The airport is operated by the Irish Airports Authority, Aer Rianta, which is responsible for the three airports of Dublin, Cork and Shannon. As the principal hub of air traffic in the Irish Republic, Dublin has been a profit-earner for the Authority, and contributed in 1980 to Aer Rianta's surplus of £2.5 million.

For the future a prime requirement will be the rebuilding of the runways at Dublin, which have been shown to be in need of improvement work because of the heavy traffic. Consequently a new major runway building programme is planned, and at least one new runway will be built, while plans for two runways have been prepared, with land acquired for them. No decision has been made as yet as to the location of the new runway in relation to the terminal building.

On other fronts, the Authority plans to expand the check-in and baggage handling facilities at Dublin, a second loading pier will be brought into use on a full-time basis and other terminal development work will be carried out. The airport, meanwhile, continues to earn profits for Aer Rianta, and in 1981 a £5 million surplus was expected.

Operated by the Irish Airports Authority, which is responsible also for Cork and Shannon airports, Dublin Airport's traffic is now approximating three million passengers a year, or about the same as Lisbon.

Dusseldorf

West Germany

Location: 4 miles north of Dusseldorf
Elevation: 144ft (44m)
Runways in use: 2
06/24 9,840ft×150ft (3,000m×45m)
16/34 5,347ft×165ft (1,630m×50m)
Passengers handled in 1981: 7,350,000
Total aircraft movements in 1981: 113,000
Cargo handled in 1981: 32,000 tonnes

Like so many of the airports in Germany, Dusseldorf was first activated as a flying field by the use of airships, and in September 1909 the first Zeppelin paid a call to what was later to become an airship base. In 1912 the Zeppelin *Schwaben* was housed at the site, and by 1913 these aerial giants were joined by the first biplanes.

It was not until 1927, however, that the site north of the city and just a few kilometres from the River Rhine saw its first duty as an airport, when in April 1927 the first airline services began by the forerunner of the present Lufthansa. The succeeding years saw a range of now-historic types of aircraft use the airport with bigger and heavier passenger loads, and among them was the Junkers F13, said to be the world's first all-metal civil aeroplane and of

which type Lufthansa once owned 50 aircraft. The F13 was followed by types such as the Messerschimitt M18, the M20, the Dornier *Merkur* and the gaint Junkers G38.

As the aircraft grew, so did the airport, until the time of World War II when it was taken over for military purposes. By now the city's airport had an attractive clutch of buildings, a spacious flying field which had been used regularly by numerous international airlines, and an open air restaurant which attracted many visitors in the summer months.

The first postwar services were made to the rebuilt airport in April 1949 when British European Airways began a service from Northolt and linking Hamburg. Scandinavian Airlines followed with services betwen Dusseldorf and Copenhagen, and KLM, SABENA and Air France then joined them. US operators American Overseas Airlines and Pan American introduced services in September 1950.

With the commencement of services by the reborn Lufthansa in 1955, Dusseldorf once again

The progressive development plan for Dusseldorf Airport is evident from this picture.

began to take its place as a German air transport facility, and like its national airline, has been expanding steadily ever since. it was not until the 1960s however, that a new terminal development scheme and airport expansion programme got under way, and this terminal development programme is still in train, on a phased basis.

A number of design ideas had been drawn up in the 1950s, one of these, in 1952, providing for a long, single terminal in the centre of two parallel runways, and which would have provided parking places for aircraft on either side and under a canopied roof after the fashion of Berlin's famous Tempelhof Airport, now closed. Another design, conceived in 1955, envisaged a half-circle passenger terminal with control tower on the inside of this circle. The design was interesting because it considered remoted square terminal buildings, space out over a very large apron aginst which individual aircraft parked. Passengers would have presumably reached these terminal halls by underground passageways from the main building.

These various designs were abandoned in favour of the present design, which has a central terminal building fronted by a trident-like complex of three piers, after the shape of a compressed W. Work on this design was put in hand in 1967, the airport's 40th anniversary year, and terminal construction work begun in February 1969. The new central

Two familiar German airlines — Lufthansa and LTU — are pictured at the important hub of Dusseldorf, and which has had a flying field since 1909.

terminal was begun in May 1971. Under the first phase of this terminal scheme the central prong of the fork was built and the northerly pier, together with the main terminal structure and an adjoining multi-storey carpark building. The southerly pier will be built as traffic requirements dictate.

With the central pier surmounted by a circular, three-level control tower, the overall design is both attractive and interesting. Both the central apron and northerly pier areas provide parking spaces for no fewer than 22 large aircraft, at nose-in positions. These aircraft are served by articulated passenger airbridges linked to the terminals. Other parking places provide for a further 28 aircraft.

The express railway, operating between Dusseldorf Airport and the main station since 1975, was extended for 19km in 1980 into the south-eastern catchment area as far as Solingen-Ohlings.

In 1981 Dusseldorf Airport inaugurated a second parking lot with some 1,000 spaces, as well as a hangar for winter service vehicles. The cost of both projects was DM25 million.

A new mission control centre, covering flight information, distribution, ramp, staff and equipment control will be available from January 1982.

Edinburgh (Turnhouse)   UK

Location: 7 miles west of Edinburgh, Scotland
Elevation: 135ft (41m)
Runways in use: 3
07/25 8,400ft×150ft (2,560m×45m)
13/31 6,000ft×150ft (1,829m×45m)
08/26 3,455ft×150ft (1,053m×45m)
Airport area: 901 acres
Passengers handled in 1981: 1,120,600
Total aircraft movements in 1981: 23,900
Cargo handled in 1981: 900 tonnes

Scotland's principal city gained a new airport on 27 May 1977 when the redeveloped airport at Turnhouse was put into commission with a spanking new terminal and runway. The new terminal was

opened by HM the Queen, and this terminal is designed to accommodate up to 1.5 million passengers a year. The development work cost £15 million.

There has been an airfield at Turnhouse since 1915, when the Royal Flying Corps used the base for training, and the field remained an air force site until 1960, when RAF Fighter Command handed over control to the Ministry of Civil Aviation. It was, however, already seeing commercial air services, for British European Airways use it from 1947, and air transport operations were carried on progressively through the 1950s. The main runway was extended and strengthened, and a new terminal built in 1956.

This terminal was subsequently enlarged, but the airport facilities in general were inadequate for the significant growth experienced in the late 1950s and early 1960s, and further development was clearly needed. Lengthy negotiation between the Government, Edinburgh Corporation and the British Airports Authority led to the transfer of ownership to the BAA in April 1971. The conditions of this transfer included a government grant to cover 75% of the cost of a new runway and terminal complex to meet future needs, and it is this development which has just recently been completed. The new runway was opened in April 1976 and it joins two others which between them are now handling 26,000 movements a year.

Work has now begun in extending the international departure lounge, and this work, costing some £400,000, was scheduled to have been completed in 1982.

Scotland's capital city airport is a major stop on the London-Scotland Shuttle service.

Frankfurt (Rhein/Main)

West Germany

Location: 5 miles SW of Frankfurt
Elevation: 568ft (173m)
Runways in use: 2
07L/25R 12,792ft×200ft (3,900m×60m)
07R/25L 12,300ft×150ft (3,750m×45m)
Airport area: 2,982 acres
Passengers handled in 1981: 17,718,537
Total air transport movements in 1981: 221,037
Cargo handled in 1981: 634,494 tonnes

Plans for flying from what was to become the great Frankfurt Airport were first laid in 1924, when on 2 July the predecessor of the present Flughafen Frankfurt/Main AG (Frankfurt/Main Airport Company) was founded. This company was called Sudwestdeutsche Luftverkehrs (SWL), and the initial capital was some DM 400,000. The aim of the company was the promotion of public aviation and the construction of airports and airship terminals, an ambitious philosphy for the time, but one which seems to have reflected much foresight; one of the most active international airport planning and engineering consultancies today is Flughafen Frankfurt AG.

In the 1930s Frankfurt was the site of numerous Zeppelin operations and the Luftschiffbau Zeppelin GmbH was based there. In 1934 and 1935 greater attention was given to the German airships than to fixed-wing aeroplanes, for at that time the large ocean-ranging gas-filled Zeppelins seemed to hold greater promise for international flights than did the aeroplane. After a number of airship disasters, however, the aeroplane took over and Frankfurt became an aerodrome for aeroplanes alone.

In 1935 work began on the construction of the Rhein/Main airport, on the site occupied by the airport today. Then it occupied 1,580 acres, however, and now it covers 2,982 acres. On 8 July 1936 a Junkers Ju52 of Deutsche Lufthansa landed at the airport and this signalled the commencement of airliner flights. In the summer of 1937 27

Frankfurt Airport is the busiest in the West German airport network, and one of the most important in Europe. It is also fourth busiest cargo airport in the world.

destinations could be reached from Frankfurt Airport, and the number was expanding steadily. The war stopped commercial air services, however, and it was not until May 1945, when American troops took over the airfield, that a programme of rebuilding was begun to turn the site once again into a commercial airport.

On 18 May 1946 an aircraft of American Overseas Airlines became the first civil transport to land at Frankfurt since the war, and three months later SAS commenced the first scheduled service, covering Copenhagen to Marseilles by way of Frankfurt. Two years later, in 1948, the importance of the airport grew with the operation of the Berlin Airlift, and later this importance was strengthened when world's first jet airliner, the Comet 1, entered service for the first hard runways that had been laid were now a necessity.

In February 1950 the airport had been given the new official name of Frankfurt Rhein/Main Airport, and the first development work to expand the facility into a major air transport hub was carried out. This development programme culminated in a massive scheme for transforming the airport, which was begun in the 1960s with the construction of a new arrivals and departures building. A feature of this was a new domestic traffic lounge, in 1963, and then in 1964 a large-scale fuel storage facility was erected. In 1965 the foundation stone for the new central terminal was laid, and this was to be put into service in March 1972, after one of the largest construction programmes in the Federal German Republic.

Deutsche Lufthansa, once again one of the world's major airlines, has extensive facilities at Frankfurt, including its cargo headquarters, where a new automated cargo terminal has been built. Because of this work, and because Frankfurt is the main gateway airport to the Federal Republic, it has become the busiest cargo airport in Europe. From the passenger viewpoint Frankfurt/Main is now equipped to handle over 30 million passengers a year.

Because 80% of West Germany's international traffic is handled at Frankfurt a third, westerly, runway has been needed for some time, to answer the landing needs of the 100-plus airlines that use thr airport . This runway is scheduled to be built and brought into service in the early 1980s, when all environmental objections have been met.

Gatwick   UK

Location: 28 miles south of London
Elevation: 202ft (62m)
Runways in use: 1
08/26 10,165ft × 150ft (3,098m × 45m)
Airport area: 1,876 acres
Passengers handled in 1981: 10,730,000
Total aircraft movements in 1981: 125,073
Cargo handled in 1981: 132,523 tonnes

If terminal facilities were the criteria for an airport to become established as an international air hub, Gatwick would be accepted the world over, for the airport can match the best of such airports on six continents. Equally, the traffic at this London airport is already impressive. Currently handling almost 11 million passengers a year, the new facilities at Gatwick have a capacity for 16 million and an ultimate capacity of 25 million.

Gatwick began life as a private aerodrome in August 1930 on a site about a mile south of the present terminal. In 1934 the first public licence was issued to the operators, a company called Airports Limited, and the first moves towards development were made. The first development scheme included the construction of a circular terminal known as the Beehive, and the airport managers introduced the novel idea of having the airliners of the day taxi up to this building and partk around it at designated places. Passengers reached the aircraft by walking through one of the six short covered walkways, a concept which might be said to have been the first pier system functioning from a radial terminal in England and possibly Europe.

In this form the airport was officially opened for air transport flights on 6 June 1936 by the Secretary of State for Air, Viscount Swinton. The war years saw Gatwick requisitioned by the Air Ministry, and in 1946 the RAF indicated that it would relinquish the use of the airport, but the de-requisitioning was deferred, and by June 1947 the Ministry of Civil Aviation had prepared a memorandum to the effect that Gatwick might be developed as a future London airport. As Heathrow had already been chosen as the principal London Airport, Gatwick's future remained uncertain.

By July 1952 announcement was made in Parliament of the Government's decision to develop Gatwick as an alternative to London Airport, and from then on the scene was set for a run-up to development of the airport according to a postwar Stage 1 scheme. Under this scheme a box-like terminal with a single 900ft long pier was built on a site to the north of the original Beehive (which still stands today), and a 7,000ft long runway laid.

This brand new airport, which cost under £7 million to build, was adequate until 1962, when Heathrow was already showing signs of strain from charter and holiday traffic. It was then decided to implement a Stage II scheme, which involved construction of two more piers, laterally disposed to the terminal, and the expansion of the terminal building to about double its previous size. The runway was lengthened to 8,200ft and the apron doubled in area.

Recognising the potential of the airport in the wake of the fiasco over the creation of a third London airport, eventually abandoned, the Government planners approved a third development scheme, and in May 1974 the first phase of this work was completed with the construction of an internationae arrivals terminal. The first phase, which saw installation of substantial advanced equipment, was followed by completion of the second phase eight months later. Under this work a brand new multi-

storey car park was built on the other side of the
main London railway line, which connects with the
airport, a new catering suite including a restaurant,
banqueting area and cocktail lounge, and a linking
bridge, equipped with travelator, constructed to join
the new car park to the main terminal.

This third stage of development was scheduled to
cost £70 million, and provided for the later
replacement of the original central pier by a new pier,
equipped with moving walkways, airbridges and air
conditioned gate rooms, and the construction of a
new cargo centre to the north of the single runway.
After expenditure of £100 million, Stage III was
completed with the opening in November 1977 of
the new central pier. This provides for 11 parking
stands for wide-bodied aircraft, with provision for
four more parking places on the apron. With the
complementary north and south piers, parking
stands in the terminal area are raised to some 27 in
total.

With this development work passenger capacity
at Gatwick has been raised to 16 million passengers/

*Gatwick Airport is now fourth busiest international
airport in the world, which is a remarkable position
for a single runway airport.*

year. In its new form Gatwick is a fine airport and
very different to the charter-flight airport of the
1950s. The problem for the British Airports
Authority, which owns and manages the airport has
been to persuade airlines which use Heathrow to
move to Gatwick and transfer some or all of their
services to London's second airport. Thirty scheduled
airlines now use the airport.

The surge in airline interest in Gatwick in 1981-
82 led to further pressure on the pace of
development work. The central pier now has stands
for 11 aircraft, and modernisation was begun of the
south pier. A new satellite terminal was due for
completion in 1983, and this will accommodate
eight large aircraft. A rapid transit system will carry
passengers to and from the main terminal.

By 1982, Gatwick had become the fourth busiest
international airport in the world — officially.

Geneva (Cointrin)   Switzerland

Location: 2.5 miles from Geneva city centre
Elevation: 1,410ft (430m)
Runways in use: 1
05/23 12,792ft×164ft (3,900m×50m)
Passengers handled in 1981: 4,774,861
Total aircraft movements in 1981: 124,806
Cargo handled in 1981: 32,700 tonnes

The efficiency of the Swiss is internationally recognised, and there are various manifestations of this efficiency in Swiss air transport, as exemplified by Swissair, the national airline, which moves cautiously but almost always does well annually, the KSSU partnership, of which Swissair was a prime mover, and the Swiss airport system, which effectively handles an important traffic while generally managing to overcome all of the noise, environmental and communications problems that might be expected in a small, high-income country such as Switzerland.

There are no more than half a dozen principal air transport airports in Switzerland, and Geneva is ranked second to Zurich amongst these in terms of passenger traffic and airline movements. Geneva-Cointrin is handling about 37% of all Swiss airport traffic, and with a throughput now of over four million passengers annually it takes its place among the favoured European air ports of call.

The airport's efficiency was becoming stretched by 1965, when a growing tide of smaller airlines were using the airport every year on holiday charter flights, to the relief of Zurich and the further betterment of the Swiss economy, but to the mild anxiety of the airport authorities. They were aware that Cointrin was ill-equipped to handle the big new aircraft that were on the drawing boards, should they become a reality (the Boeing 747 was ordered first in 1966).

In was in 1965, therefore, that the Geneva Cantonal authorities decided to institute a modernisation programme which would not only reshape the airport but which would be bold enough to provide for all kinds of aircraft and their traffic for a long time to come.

For Geneva Airport, this was not the first modernisation plan that had been implemented. The city of Geneva had had an airport since 1920, when an air route between Cointrin and Paris had been inaugurated, and in 1944 a new concrete runway was laid to prepare for the postwar traffic. The grass strip and wooden huts of 1922 gave way in 1945 to a postwar improvement scheme, but since that time there had not been a development programme of such magnitude — or cost.

The dramatic new plan of 1965 called for tunnels and a system of satellite terminals linked with the main terminal, to keep the apron clear for very large aircraft. The Geneva plan made obsolete the former terminal building, with its now-quaint arrangement for travellers to walk across the apron to board the aircraft in any weather. A new system of roads was also required, together with a hydrant fuelling system, passenger conveyors and escalators, and clearly-defined direction flows. Most importantly, the satellite terminals would be unlike anything the airport had ever had before, and would, in fact, come to serve as a model design concept for many other international airports, although the last feature was not thought of greatly at the time.

Brought to reality in 1968 (two years before the Boeing 747 began operations), the Geneva plan introduced the first remoted satellite terminal system

Geneva's Cointrin Airport is notable for its three circular satellite terminals, which are linked to the main terminal by underground passageway.

to any European airport. With this arrangement three radial terminals were positioned on the apron, some way from the main terminal by which passengers depart from the airport and make their way to Geneva and environs when arriving at it.

The radial satellites act as holding lounges for passengers after completing check-in and other procedures in the main terminal, and for the passenger the decision was generally quickly made to take the conveyor along the underground passageway to the terminal and his aircraft parked alongside it. The option is open to remain in the main terminal until departure time, but this is not easy if the traveller sees his aircraft taxi in — or believes he does. For the airport authority the satellite terminal idea was perfect insofar as it cleared the main terminal of languishing passengers to make more room for processing procedures.

For the future at Geneva, there is the 'Horizon 2000' plan, which will bring into play bifurcated pier extensions to the main terminal, to join the satellite buildings.

Now there is a further development plan in hand for Geneva-Cointrin, to take the airport traffic to 8 million passengers a year by 1990, and up to 10 million by the end of the century. For 1990, a 'Y'-shaped terminal will be built extending from the main terminal complex, and this will be joined by a second, fellow structure for the 'Horizon 2000' plan.

Swiss national carrier Swissair is unique amongst world airlines at the time of writing for its orders for the newest models of the Airbus (A310), the B747 (SUD) and the extended range DC-10-30ER. It also has a large fleet of DC-9-80s, seen here at Geneva.

Hamburg (Fuhlsbuttel)

West Germany

Location: 5 miles north of Hamburg
Elevation: 52ft (16m)
Runways in use: 3
05/23 10,660ft × 150ft (3,250m × 45m)
16/34 12,020ft × 150ft (3,665m × 45m)
05/23 3,936ft × 165ft (1,200m × 50m) (grass)
Passengers handled in 1981: 4,528,202
Total aircraft movements in 1981: 98,841
Cargo handled in 1981: 55,722 tonnes

There has been flying at Hamburg, North Germany, since 1908, and while this flying began with balloons, such was the development of this form of aerial transport that airship hangars were established there in 1912, and the Graf Zeppelin operated from the airfield, which has been claimed to be 'the first airport in Europe'.

Because of the importance of the city of Hamburg, Hamburg Airport became important too, and in the 1920s the national airline Lufthansa carried on many of its international services from there. The airport was later used for military purposes, and the postwar years then saw development of the site at Fuhlsbuttel, just five miles from the city, to the stature of the present day. Lufthansa has also made the airport its Technical Base, and amongst other things, the airline has aircraft overhaul and engine test facilities at the airport.

The terminal complex at Hamburg is after the traditional design of the prewar period, but this has of course undergone much modification in recent times. A curved central terminal looks out over a wide apron on which the aircraft are parked, and the terminal is fronted by a canopied structure beneath which passengers join their aircraft. Flanking the central terminal are two wing buildings which are

provided with telescoping airbridges to support the traffic flow. The landside of the terminal is fronted by the Zeppelinstrasse, a main road passing the airport, and between this road and the terminal there is extensive car parking space. Such is the traffic at Hamburg that provision for long-term parking has been made on the other side of the Zeppelinstrasse also, to provide 1,827 open parking spaces in all. Some covered car parks are available also.

The airport is situated near the E3 Autobahn running to Flensburg and Kiel in the north and in the southerly direction to the suburbs of north-west Hamburg. To the south-west lies the city of Bremen, down the E3 Autobahn, and due south is Hanover. The airport thus plays a particularly important role in serving the north of the Federal German Republic, as well as Scandinavian countries.

Development plans for Hamburg Fuhlsbuttel were temporarily halted in 1968 when it was first announced that a new airport for Hamburg, located at Kaltenkirchen, further north of Hamburg and in the direction of Kiel, was to be built. This airport, a major project to cost many millions of DM, will have two half-circle terminal buildings, bisected by a main road which will provide for all future big jets. Construction of the airport was deferred following the fuel crisis of 1973-74, and plans for the airport stretched out. Plans for Kaltenkirchen Airport have been reactivated however, and it is now thought likely that the airport could be introduced into service some time in the 1980s.

Hamburg has been the scene of flying since 1908. The airport is expected to be replaced by a new one, but no date has been put upon that.

Helsinki (Vantaa) Finland

Helsinki (Vantaa)/Finland
Location: 12 miles from Helsinki city centre
Elevation: 167ft (51m)
Runways in use: 2
04/22 10,500ft×200ft (3,200m×60m)
15/33 9,510ft×200ft (2,900m×60m)
Airport area: 2,965 acres
Passengers handled in 1981: 3,457,608
Total aircraft movements in 1981: 55,264
Cargo handled in 1981: 27,626 tonnes

The long, hard winters of countries in the northern latitudes give air transport authorities in those countries many problems, but the Finns have had long experience in meeting these problems for they have been carrying on air services for over 55 years. As the principal airport of Helsinki, Helsinki-Vantaa was opened in 1952 just prior to the Helsinki Olympic Games, and is now seeing traffic totalling almost 3.5 million passengers a year. This traffic has been climbing steadily over the years, but had a particular boost in the mid-1970s when national airline Finnair introduced its DC-9-50 and DC-10-30 aircraft on European and transatlantic services respectively.

The original landplane airport for Helsinki was at Malmi, opened in 1936, and prior to this date Katajanokka served as the base for seaplane operations, which were carried on right in the heart of the city. Malmi was superseded for international operations in 1952 with the opening of Vantaa Airport, which is further away from the city but purpose-built for big jet operations. Its location also ensures minimum noise nuisance.

The airport is situated in the province of Vantaa, near to the Tuusula Motorway and 12 miles from the Helsinki city centre. Apart from being the principal hub of commercial air traffic in Finland. It is also the home base for most Finnish air companies and most Finnish aviation concerns. National carrier Finnair has its hangars and repair shops on the airport.

The present passenger terminal was brought into use in 1969. It serves both the scheduled domestic and international flights and charter services. The architects of Finland (notably Saarinen) have produced some elegant terminals for world airports and the terminal at Helsinki-Vantaa is no exception, with its sweeping roof and substantial areas of glass giving a wide aspect to the surrounding scene. For

the traveller, warmth and light are welcome characteristics of the terminal, which is so constructed as to give a raised view to the apron. By its design the terminal is raised well above the apron level so that departing passengers may pass from elevated roadways straight through the terminal building and down into their aircraft cabins. The first level below the terminal is given over to airport buses and service vehicles arriving for passengers, while a second lower level is given over to a car park for airline passengers.

The airport has not yet moved to such advanced aids for winter operations as heated runways, but the Vantaa fleet of snowploughs and snow-dispersing equipment is substantial and ever-active in winter conditions, and runway 22 is equipped for Category II bad weather landing operations. Both runways are equipped with low and high-intensity runway and approach lights, visual approach slope indicators and ILS facilities to ensure that the airport is constantly serviceable. Indeed, the airport authorities maintain that the airport is operational in all weather conditions, and traffic breaks have been restricted to 15 minutes at most.

The airport terminal is being extended on the international side, and the Customs Hall will be newly introduced by the end of 1982. A separate terminal has recently been built for general aviation.

Helsinki's Vantaa Airport sees a fair cargo traffic. This is the cargo terminal, used primarily by Finnair.

The main terminal at Helsinki was brought into use in 1969.

Hong Kong (Kai Tak)

Hong Kong

Location: Kowloon peninsula, 3 miles from Victoria
Elevation: 15ft (4.5m)
Runways in use: 1
13/31 11,130ft×200ft (3,390m×60m)
Passengers handled in 1981: 7,108,774
Total aircraft movements in 1981: 53,841
Cargo handled in 1981: 258,627 tonnes
Airport area: 530 acres

The British Crown Colony of Hong Kong consists of 236 islands and islets and a portion of the Chinese mainland east of the Pearl River estuary. The total area of this land is 398¼sq miles. The principal city of Hong Kong is Victoria and, facing Hong Kong Island is the Kowloon peninsula, where Kai Tak Airport is situated. Kowloon Bay is closely encircled on the landward side by high hills and the approaches over these to the airport are very poor. The mountainous nature of the region makes it a hazardous one for the airline pilots, and the idea of making long shallow approaches by big jets over this route is out of the question.

The city had an airport from 1929, when the newly formed Hong Kong Flying Club rented part of the land reclaimed from Kowloon Bay for its landing field. The field was developed into an airport, and by 1932 1,185 passengers had been flown from it. The Government then took over construction and operation of this site, and civil flying was put on to a money-making basis. In 1936 Imperial Airways began a weekly service between Hong Kong and Penang to connect with the England-Australia flights. By the end of the same year Pan American had opened another route, between Hong Kong and the United States, using flying-boats which landed on the waters of Kowloon Bay.

During World War II the airport was used by the Japanese as a strategic air base, and considerably enlarged. In the postwar period it was not until 1947 that the airport began to take its place in international air operations. It then had two runways, but their length and the general arrangement of the site were considered limited, and after much discussion the Hong Kong Government decided that a completely new airport would have to be built on the existing site.

In 1954 work on this new airport was approved and then began one of the biggest airport construction schemes undertaken in Asia. The principal feature of this project was the construction of the runway, for to overcome the problems caused by the surrounding mountains, it was to be built actually out into Kowloon Bay, stretching for 8,350ft from the mainland over the water. The project was remarkable feat of engineering and construction work, and took 2½ years to complete. It involved the use of 20 million tons of material, including 11 million tons of filling, and the efforts of 3,000 workers daily. It cost the Hong Kong Government some $135 million, and was introduced into service in 1958.

Initially, this runway was made 8,350ft long and 200ft wide, and stressed to take aircraft weights of

Control tower at Hong Kong Airport, which watches over 55,000 air transport movements a year.

up to 450,000lb, but this length was extended to 10,000ft in the 1970s, when the first Boeing B747s began to operate.

Since this time, Kai Tak Airport has become even more important to international air transport as passenger traffic has increased from 1.5 to over 7 million travellers a year, and substantial terminal expansion work has been required — and the runway lengthened yet again. A new terminal building was opened in November 1962, and an extension to the departures hall built in August 1977; a similar extension was made to the arrivals hall in early 1978.

The passenger terminal is now handling more than 5,000 passengers an hour in peak periods, and to speed this traffic flow a semi-automatic baggage system, with computerised sorting, has been installed. The access roads to and from the airport have been improved, and the air traffic services provided with the latest equipment. An instrument landing system was commissioned in 1974, and secondary surveillance radar recently installed. In August 1977 a sequenced strobe lighting system was brought into operation to provide improved visual guidance at night and in poor visibility for landing aircraft.

With 31 international airlines providing 960 scheduled passenger services to and from Hong Kong each week, the single runway is now seeing a heavy annual utilisation, and by way of improving this runway further it was given additional length of up to 11,130ft, which became available at the end of

1975. Concurrently, construction was completed on a road tunnel under the north-west end of the runway. Such tunnelling work has benefited the movement of surface traffic to and from the airport and around it; the cross-harbour tunnel, which was opened in 1972, brought the airport to within a 15-minute drive of Hong Kong Island.

Apart from its passenger traffic, Kai Tak is one of the busiest cargo airports in Asia, and a new cargo complex was opened at the airport in 1976 with an ultimate handling capability of 500,000 tons. This cargo facility is financed and operated by Hong Kong Air Cargo Terminals Limited, a consortium comprising the Hong Kong Government and four local organisations.

As fascinating as it already is, the story of Kai Tak Airport is taking a new turn, for indications are the airport may become saturated for practical purposes by 1985. The next move will be a replacement airport for the Colony, and in order to provide for this, the Civil Aviation Department of Hong Kong commissioned a plan for a replacement airport for Kai Tak in 1979, and this plan was completed in April 1980. In the report, the consultants up-dated traffic forecasts, and confirmed the feasibility of constructing and operating an airport on a proposed site at Chek Lap Kok. This island is located off the north-west coast of Lantao Island, and west of the Hong Kong mainland. The consultants also advised on the noise impact of operating the proposed replacement airport on a 24-hour basis; and this was considered acceptable.

Based on the findings of the consultancy study, the Director of Civil Aviation proposed to the government that further detailed studies be carried out. The Master Plan study covered all aspects of the proposed replacement airport, including transport infrastructure and environmental matters. The Master Plan study, commenced on 1 March 1981, and scheduled to take some two years, was being carried out by the Ralph M. Parsons International company of Pasadena, California. It is the expectation of the Hong Kong DCA that results of the study will be made available at the beginning of 1983, whereupon the Hong Kong Government will be asked to give a decision on whether or not to proceed with the construction of the project.

The proposed airport, to be located on the small island of Chek Lap Kok, would be a twin-runway facility with both runways very largely built on land reclaimed from the sea, in the same manner that Kai Tak currently operates. There would be road and rail links connecting with Lantao Island and the Hong Kong mainland. Chek Lap Kok is a 580-acre island, or not dissimilar to Kai Tak's current 530 acres. More airport land will be made available by reclamation however, if the project goes ahead, for Tung Chung Bay will disappear in the reclamation work. Plans provide also for the new airport to be linked to the western part of the New Territories mainland by means of a coastal highway, and fast hovercraft and helicopter services may also be included in the new airport facilities.

Britain's British Airports Authority is expected to play a part in the study work, together with the Royal Observatory, which has been carrying out meteorological and oceanographic studies.

The proposed replacement airport could be built in two phases, the first phase, estimated to cost HK$5,500 million, will have one runway of 3,600m length. The second phase, costing some HK$1,700 million, would involve construction of the second runway, at 2,800m length. If the Hong Kong Government decides to proceed with the project, construction work would start in 1984, and Phase 1 would be ready for use by 1990.

Hong Kong's Kai Tak Airport is so pressed with traffic that a new airport should be built. Main terminal complex is seen here.

Honolulu International   USA

Location: On the Island of Oahu, Hawaii
Elevation: 13ft (4m)
Runways in use: 4
8L/26R 12,360ft × 150ft (3,745m × 45m)
8R/26L 12,000ft × 200ft (3,636m × 61m)
4L/22R 6,948ft × 200ft (2,105m × 61m)
4R/22L 9,000ft × 150ft (2,727m × 45m)
Passengers handled in 1981: 14,344,200
Air transport movements in 1981: 198,400
Cargo handled in 1981: 166,400 tons

The interestingly-located — and very busy — airport of Honolulu International is one of some 14 air bases in the eight main islands which constitute Hawaii, and Honolulu is also the main international airport for the group. Operated by the State of Hawaii Department of Transportation's Airport Division, Honolulu adjoins the US Air Force base of Hickam Field, and is flanked by the famous Pearl Harbor.

One of the world's water-based international airports, Honolulu is on the edge of Mamala Bay, and not far from the famous Waikiki Beach and Diamond Head; it is only a few miles from the Honolulu business district.

Oahu is the third most northerly island in the Hawaiian group, with the largest and the main island of Hawaii being the most southerly. For visitors, the airport thus serves as a good point for reaching any of the other islands, several of which have airfields and several of them jet airports.

Passenger traffic at Honolulu has been climbing steadily, and from the 7.6 million of a decade ago in 1971, traffic increased to 8.7 million in 1972 and 11.3 million in 1976. In 1981 it was up to 14.3 million.

When it is understood that much of this traffic is tourist traffic, the steady increases can be appreciated. Figures are not available on the sums of money taken into the islands by these large numbers of tourists, but it is doubtful whether there is any shortfall of funds for necessary airport development work.

Hawaii has an imposing main central terminal flanked by further terminals to the east and west, and equipped with the familiar piers with airside parking positions. These face a pair of parallel runways, the main one of which is 8L/26R, which has over 12,000ft of operational length. This parallel pair is bisected by a further pair of shorter runways.

The airport has a general aviation area, freight centre, aircraft maintenance area, and a base for the Hawaii National Air Guard. Between the runways is the Keehi Lagoon wherein there are relocated habitats for birds. Seemingly this provision for some of the bird life of the Pacific does not represent a threat to aircraft operations.

Honolulu Airport, in the beautiful state of Hawaii, is another truly water-based airport.

Houston Intercontinental   USA

Location: 17 miles north of Houston city centre
Elevation: 98ft (30m)
Runways in use: 2
14/32 12,000ft×150ft (3,658m×45m)
8L/26R 9,400ft×150ft (2,865m×45m)
Airport area: 8,000 acres
Passengers handled in 1981: 11,601,300
Total air transport movements in 1981: 176,400
Cargo handled in 1981: 76,600 tons

The world at large knows Houston, Texas, as the centre for Mission Control in the US space programme, and it is right therefore that the city has a space-age airport, imposing in its architecture and style. Houston has had an airport for many years, of course, since the 1920s, and the original facility started as a cow pasture to the south-east of the city. That grand facility was named the Municipal Airport, and was renamed the William P. Hobby Airport, after a local notable, in 1967 by which time a new airport for Houston was well into construction.

The first study to assess the city's future air transport needs was made in 1957, when big jet transports were on the horizon and Hobby Airport was acknowledged to be size-limited. Population and industry growth in Houston and the Texas Gulf Coast area was outpacing the development of air transport facilities, and the survey stressed the importance of the airport's keeping pace. A holding company called the Jet Era Ranch Company was founded as a medium through which 3,000 acres of land could be bought by a group of citizens of Houston for the sole purpose of resale to the city at the cost to them. This was the one way that accumulated land parcels could be acquired without long arguments over rights to oil or gas fields, highways, pipelines etc. In June 1960 the city council received full title to the 3,000 acres for development into a new airport. Additional land acquisitions, completed or in progress, then brought the total airport site to 7,300 acres. Ground-breaking began in 1962, and that year the Federal Aviation Administration selected Houston as the site for a major air route traffic control centre. The airport was officially opened for service on 1 June 1969 as Houston Intercontinental Airport. The William P. Hobby Airport is still used as a Texas regional airport and because of the demand for air transport in Texas, is to be given a $36 million 'facelift'.

Houston Intercontinental is today handling 11 million passengers a year from two runways and three terminals. The two square-shaped terminals are positioned in the centre of a long, wide strip of land with concourses projecting from each corner. The concourses, which are in effect circular holding lounges with aircraft parking places around them, are linked to the main terminals by passenger bridges. The central strip of land is so laid out as to provide for a complete doubling in size of the whole facility, in a linear expansion plan. The master plan provided for this development, and the construction of a further two box terminals with their associate concourses. The central strip provides for car parking and the free movement of passengers through the terminal halls, to the restaurants and elsewhere. The apron is all around, and the central island is reached by subterranean driveways and an underground train. A $12 million hotel, the Host Hotel, is located in the centre of the terminal building complex.

There are three air cargo buildings at the airport. Construction of a third terminal was recently completed, and this terminal, Terminal C, cost $114 million, and enables the airport to handle an additional 5.5 million passengers a year. By the end of the century Houston could be handling 69 million passengers.

Handling almost 12 million passengers annually, Houston Intercontinental currently ranks as twelfth busiest in the world.

Istanbul (Yesilkoy)   Turkey

Location: 15 miles west of Istanbul
Elevation: 92ft (28m)
Runways in use: 2
06/24 7,545ft×200ft (2,300m×60m)
18/36 9,840ft×150ft (3,000m×45m)
Passengers handled in 1981: 2,418,300
Total aircraft movements in 1981: 35,900
Cargo handled in 1981: 23,000 tonnes

Located in the heart of the Middle East between the Mediterranean and Black Seas, Turkey's geographical position is of great interest to business and tourist travellers alike. From a business point of view it represents an important hub at the eastern end of the Mediterranean, and for tourists the country holds cultural treausures representing a history which goes back thousands of years.

The two principal airports in the country are the capital city airport for Ankara (qv) and the airport for Istanbul, Yesilkoy. Of the two, Istanbul is by far the

Istanbul Airport — Yesilkoy — is the busiest airport in Turkey.

busiest handling twice the traffic annually of Ankara, and this airport is also the base for most foreign airlines serving Turkey together with national carrier Turkish Airlines (THY).

Yesilkoy was opened in 1953, and is a fairly sizeable airport designed in the conventional mould. It is located 15 miles from the city of Istanbul. It is currently seeing some 50,000 aircraft movements a year. A substantial amount of domestic airline traffic is flown within Turkey, and in the case of Yesilkoy, this domestic traffic is amounting to 635,000 passengers annually. Such busyness is a reflection of the preference for flying in this mountainous country.

The size of the airport, together with the climate have shaped the philosophy that passengers may walk across the apron to the parked aircraft without the need for boarding bridges. This apron at Yesilkoy has a capacity for three DC-10 and nine B707-types at one time.

For the future, Yesilkoy is to be given a brand new airport, which will have four terminal units eventually, each with a capacity for five million passengers a year. Terminal unit 1 was to be introduced about 1981.

Jeddah (King Abdulaziz International)   Saudi Arabia

Location: 12 miles north of Jeddah
Elevation: 58ft (17.5m)
Runways in use: 2
10,890ft × 150ft (3,300m × 45m)
12,540ft × 150ft (3,800m × 45m)
Passengers handled in 1981: 7,220,000
Cargo handled in 1981: 75,753 tonnes

Built just 19km to the north of Jeddah, Saudi Arabia, is the brand new airport of King Abdulaziz International, said to be the largest airport in the world, covering an area of 40.5 square miles.

However much of this site is taken up by the airport's facilities, the new airport for Jeddah is a most remarkable facility, built in the desert under the authority of the Saudi Arabian International Airports Projects Division, and the SA Ministry of Defence. It comprises two commercial passenger terminals, 40 mobile lounge gates, a separate terminal for Haj pilgrims travelling to Mecca, and a royal pavilion for members of the Saudi Royal Family and visiting heads of State. There are parking facilities for 44 large aircraft on the commercial aprons and another 34 at the Haj Terminal. There are South and North Terminals for domestic and international flights carried by Saudia and foreign flag carriers, and the South Terminal has 40 mobile lounge gates; there are 14 at the North Terminal. There are 10 gates at the Haj Terminal.

Additionally in this complex are two service restaurants together with coffee bars and snack counters, newsstands, banks and the usual range of shops. A post office and long-distance operator-assisted telephone services are also available, as are passenger information desks, computerised information displays, hotel reservation facilities and car rental desks. Passengers in transit have separate restaurants and lounges available for them.

There are bus services providing regular runs to the city and also to Mecca, Medina and Taif. The Saudi Limousine Company offers air-conditioned Chevrolet taxis driven by bilingual chauffeurs. Service between the South and North Terminals for interlining passengers is provided by the airport authority at no charge.

The remarkable facility that is the new Jeddah International Airport has also what is said to be the largest air cargo facility in the Middle East, with parking space for seven wide-bodied aircraft, and which can handle 150,000 tons of freight a year and store 7,500 tons at any one time, including 800 tons in cold storage.

The main terminal at the airport is a dramatically distinctive building constructed with an arabesque roof line; this is matched by the Haj Terminal, which occupies about 370 acres, and which has been constructed in the style of desert tents, with each roof of the 210 terminal tents rising conically to an open support ring in the centre. The terminal stands 10 storeys high, and each tent stands on storeys off the terminal floor. This impressive design has been fashioned after the tents of the desert to make the many thousands of annual pilgrims to Mecca feel at

home. The air traffic control building co-ordinates air traffic control information throughout the Arabian Peninsula, while the control tower itself stands 60m tall (200ft).

Development of the King Abdulaziz Airport is still in train, and from the calculated passenger traffic of 7.2 million for 1981, 10.4 million passengers are expected by 1985 and 17 million by the year 2000. For the future there will be a maintenance and overhaul base for Saudia, the national airline, a general aviation complex, a hospital and quarantine facilities, an airport administration building and an air mail terminal.

The new King Abdulaziz Airport at Jeddah is said to be the biggest in the world. This is the Hadj Terminal, especially designed for the pilgrims to Mecca, and which has a roof made of Fibreglass coated with Teflon.

The south terminal of King Abdulaziz International serves domestic and international passengers for Saudia, the national carrier. In the foreground is a mosque. Main passenger terminal is at rear.

Jersey (Channel Islands)   UK

Location: 6 miles WNW of St Helier
Elevation: 276ft (84m)
Runways in use: 1
09/27 5,595ft × 150ft (1,706m × 45m)
Airport area: 332 acres
Passengers handled in 1981: 1,304,242
Total aircraft movements in 1981: 78,734
Cargo handled in 1981: 8,271 tonnes

The Channel Islands airport of Jersey is an important one because of its great number of air transport movements every year. The airport has the greatest number of total movements annually among all of the UK airports with the exception of the two London airports, Heathrow and Gatwick. The reason for this is the large volume of holiday traffic which flies in to the attractive island year-round and places the airport among the top three UK airports.

The first air services were run to Jersey from Portsmouth to the beach in St Aubins Bay in December 1933. Regular daily flights were made to this strip by Jersey Airways, but it was hardly the place for an airport proper to be established, and the Jersey Harbours and Airport Committee looked for and found a site where a good-sized airport could be developed. This was the present site, which is situated on the Western side of the island and six miles from the principal town of St Helier. The airport is owned by the States of Jersey and administered by the Harbours and Airport Committee. The original airport had four runways, all of which were grass, and a terminal building was provided. In February 1940 a Fleet Air Arm training squadron was based at Jersey, but when the French Channel Ports were overrun commerical air services from the island

stopped, and in July 1940 the island was occupied by the Luftwaffe and the airport came under its command. From then on Jersey Airport was used by the Luftwaffe until the end of the war.

On 2 October 1945 the airport was handed back to the States of Jersey, and from then on, as the island's economy underwent a steady improvement, the airport began to see an ever rising traffic as a result of the popularity of air travel.

Various improvement works have been done at the airport in the succeeding years, culminating in the addition to the main terminal building of an international pier, which stretches across the apron to the south of the terminal building and control tower and which now provides for jet aircraft that until the mid-1960s were banned from using the airport. The new pier was opened in March 1978. Its erection had been accompanied by substantial enlargement of the apron, further lengthening of the main concrete runway to almost 6,000ft, the provision of additional hangar space and maintenance facilities, and installation of new navigational aids.

Today Jersey Airport is an important international facility and, in the peak periods between May and September, handles flights from Amsterdam, Brussels, Copenhen, Dusseldorf, Oslo and Palma, as well as eight places in France, Belfast and Dublin, and no fewer than 30 airports in Britain. On the busiest days in 1981 12,500 passengers were handled daily.

Runway and terminal layout at Jersey Airport, principal airport of the Channel Islands.

Johannesburg (Jan Smuts) South Africa

Location: 10 miles ENE of city
Elevation: 5,559ft (1,695m)
Runways in use: 2
03/21 14,495ft×200ft (4,418m×60m)
15/33 8,240ft×200ft (2,512m×60m)
Airport area: 4,555 acres
Passengers handled in 1981: 4,192,600
Total air transport movements in 1981: 59,300
Cargo handled in 1981: 114,200 tonnes

Located between the cities of Pretoria and Johannesburg, Jan Smuts Airport was opened officially in 1952 and became fully operational in September 1953. It is South Africa's main airport of entry, and as such sees a good annual traffic. In the 1930s Johannesburg had an airport at Germiston, but in those days the flying-boat was the king and less attention was given to land airports. This situation changed with the war's end and the demise of the flying-boat, and the South African Government decided to build a new airport in the late 1940s on a large plateau to the north-east of Johannesburg. With the first foundation work commenced, Field Marshal Lord Montgomery named this airport Jan Smuts, after South Africa's leader, in December 1947. Built by the South African Railways and Harbour Administration, the airport was transferred to the control of the Department of Transport and provisionally opened in April 1952. It became fully operational in September 1953 and was inaugurated on 3 October of that year.

Johannesburg's Jan Smuts Airport terminal building, fronted here by the underground car park.

Simple but functional, the Johannesburg Airport terminal is seen from the airside, with one of the national airline's B747s on the apron.

Since that time the usual development schemes have been implemented and the airport has been improved in various areas, including the passenger terminal area. It is envisaged that by the turn of the century some 45 million passengers will use the airport annually, and a development plan provides for the construction of three unit terminals, each capable of handling 10 million passengers. These will be built between a parallel runway system. The terminals will be constructed in stages, and served by a freeway road system. In the summer period the international terminal will be expanded to handle 15 million passengers a year.

Johannesburg Airport is notable for two particular features, namely its elevation which is great enough to place Jan Smuts as being amongst the highly situated airports of the world, and also the runway length, which at just under 15,000ft makes this one of the world's long runway airports, and possibly the longest in Africa.

Kansas City International

USA

Location: 15 miles NW of Kansas City
Elevation: 1,027ft (313m)
Runways in use: 2
01/19 10,800ft × 150ft (3,294m × 45m)
09/27 9,500ft × 150ft (2,895m × 45m)
Airport area: 5,600 acres
Passengers handled in 1981: 4,637,000
Total air transport movements in 1981: 128,000
Cargo handled in 1981: 23,300 tons

An historic day for Kansas City, Missouri, was 17 August 1927 for on that day Colonel Charles A. Lindbergh flew into the airport that had just been built to offically dedicate it. Fresh from his Atlantic-crossing exploit, Lindbergh was in process of making a tour of the US contingent for the promotion of aeronautics under a Guggenheim Foundation scheme. To the joy of thousands of spectators, the famous *Spirit of St Louis* circled for 15 minutes before touching down at the north end of the field.

Kansas had seen a fair amount of aviation long before this, however, for a balloon ascent was made from the heart of the city in 1869, and in 1917 the city opened its first 'airport' at a place called Holmes Road. Then in May 1926 the first airmail flight was made out of Kansas, from a place called Richards Field. By the 1940s the city in the heart of America's midwest had its own municipal airport, and with the

foresight which appears to have characterised Kansas City's aviation thinking right from the start, was already considering the idea of a magnificient new international facility, designed to serve air transport for many years to come.

By the 1950s Kansas had committed itself to a second commercial airport and purchased some land for the purpose. Trans World Airlines located its main overhaul base at the eastern edge of this field, which became called Mid-Continent Airport (later Mid-Continent International). It was felt likely that this site would become the second airport, but by 1963 the inadequacy of Kansas City Municipal Airport indicated that a completely fresh development was required, and further land, therefore, was purchased adjacent to that originally acquired for purposes of a brand new international airport. This left TWA's base at the eastern end, which the planned airport site situated to the west.

The new airport came to be called Kansas City International, or KCI, and while it took no more than four years for the construction, its history proper began in 1963 with the decision by city officials that

The imaginative concept for Kansas City International is based upon a minimum walking distance for travellers. Airport cover 5,000 acres.

airline operations would have to be moved. When the plans were finalised, it was decided that 5,000 acres would be required for the airport, or some five times that of Municipal Airport. At that time, only two airports in the United States exceeded this size: New York International Airport and San Francisco International.

The concept of KCI was based on the facts that airline travellers in the main were usually obliged to leave their cars in a car park some distance from the terminal, trudge substantial distances to the check-in point, and then walk another 1,000ft to board the aircraft. Planning for KCI dictated that irrations such as this should be eliminated as far as possible and the idea was one of 'drive-to-your-gate', by which the traveller drove to the airport, followed signs indicating his flight number or direction, and parked virtually at the terminal entrance. Leaving his car the traveller accomplished baggage check-in in a matter of minutes, and by simply walking the width of a narrow building, could board the aircraft. At KCI the distance walked is not much more than 100ft.

To achieve this bold thinking the planners of KCI surrounded the circular control tower and airport administrative centre with four massive circular terminal complexes, like wheels around a larger central wheel. Each terminal complex provides a massive central parking lot with the narrow terminal building circling its edge. On the airside of this terminal 'wheel', is the apron on which the aircraft park. These aircraft are reached by passenger airbridges after the passenger has taken the appropriate gate for his flight.

The scheme might be compared with the traditional structural pier concept, which permits multiple loading of aircraft, but it is unique in its elimination of unnecessary walking distances for the passenger. It carries the decentralisation idea almost to its ultimate and offers great passenger convenience, for amongst other things it does not involve the need for any form of passenger transfer system. As of the moment three of the four annular terminals planned have been built. Each terminal is 2,300ft long, 65ft wide and with three levels: ramp level, passenger service level and mezzanine level (incorporating a restaurant). Each terminal car park will hold 850 cars, and 920 additional spaces are located between each terminal, for longer term parking. Provision is made for multi-level parks within the terminal circles, to provide for up to 180 spaces per gate.

On the airside each terminal has 51 aircraft gate positions. There are currently two runways with provision for more as traffic expansion dictates. In its present form the airport is capable of handling up to eight million passengers a year.

Karachi

Pakistan

Location: 9 miles ENE of city
Elevation: 100ft (30m)
Runways in use: 2
07L/25R 10,500ft×150ft (3,200m×45m)
07R/25L 7,500ft×150ft (2,285m×45m)
Airport area: 1,280 acres
Passengers handled in 1980: 3,499,888
Total aircraft movements in 1980: 53,906
Cargo handled in 1980: 69,159 tonnes

Karachi Airport has an historic place in international air transport, for it served as the terminus for the England to India air service during the 1930s, and when the through route from Croydon was operated by Imperial Airways. Indeed, it was proposed to operate airship services to Karachi, but when the R101 crashed in France in October 1930 this put paid to airship services. Instead, the Handley Page 42s of Imperial Airways became the familiar aircraft operating to Karachi in the early prewar days.

As the traffic built up, hangars were erected and a small Customs building set up. By December 1938 the Governor of Sind opened a permanent terminal building, which had a circular central hall and two wing buildings, and which has still been used up to the present time. Further expansion was made to the east, and a paved runway laid, and during the 1950s the main runway, which had a length of 7,500ft, was joined by another, built slightly to the north and which was made 10,500ft long to suit jet aircraft.

In 1965 the Pakistan Department of Civil Aviation, together with state airline PIA, drew up a master plan for Karachi Airport for the future. Under this master plan a new terminal was designed, to ease the weight of fast-growing traffic at the airport, and which has risen by over four times in the past decade. While this master plan was being acted upon, PIA constructed an intermediary terminal to handle traffic for the Gulf. This terminal was made a single-storey prefabricated structure, 450ft long, with two departure lounges, one for first-class passengers and the other for economy-class and others. This terminal can handle four wide-bodied aircraft simultaneously.

The preliminary design for the new main terminal featured a two-storey building with two piers and 17 aircraft stands. Passenger handling is to be on the upper level.

The Pakistan Department of Civil Aviation has not revealed the latest progress with the master plan for the airport, which will undoubtedly undergo some modifications before its final introduction into service, but the DC's figures well illustrate the remarkable traffic growth in recent times. In 1970-71 863,000 passengers used Karachi Airport in total, and in four short years this traffic had almost doubled, to 1,430,000. By 1977 total passenger traffic was up to 2.4 million, and by 1980 another million had been added to the total passenger throughput. Cargo similarly has been growing well at Karachi, from 13,000 tons in 1970 to 37,000 tons in 1975-6 and to 69,000 tons by 1980.

Lagos International

Nigeria

Location: 8 miles north of Lagos
Elevation: 135ft (40m)
Runways in use: 1
01/19 11,975ft × 150ft (3,650m × 45m)

The main airports of Nigeria have been the subject of a large-scale development plan initiated in the 1970s, and the capital city airport at Lagos was given this modernisation treatment as a feature of this plan, culminating in the opening of a brand new airport at Lagos and named Murtala Mohammed Airport, replacing the former airport of Ijeka International. This development plan, which has been undertaken by the Dutch airport consultancy and planning consortium NACO, gave Lagos a major new terminal development complex, of several storeys, and extending over a wide area. With the Netherlands Airport Consultancy Organisation in charge of the Nigerian airport scheme, it is perhaps understandable that Murtala Mohammed Airport bears a strong resemblance to Amsterdam Schiphol

Airport, a resemblance which has been noted by visitors.

As a part of this airport development scheme, the single runway at Lagos is to be joined by a second runway, of some 3,900m length. The timescale for this runway development is not known. Terminal development work at Murtala Mohammed included further expansion of the cargo area, which facility has been extremely busy in recent years, as oil-wealthy Nigeria has been importing large quantities of materials and consumer goods as much by air as by sea, to the benefit of numerous foreign airlines, including British freighting operators.

Lagos Airport is served by some 29 airlines and is the headquarters base for the national carrier, Nigeria Airways. It is served regularly by British Caledonian Airways from Britain.

The international airport of Lagos was built according to the designs of a Dutch planning consortium, and bears a resemblance to Amsterdam Airport.

Leningrad (Shosseinaya)

USSR

Location: 9 miles south of Leningrad
Elevation: 59ft (18m)
Runways in use: 2
10/31 8,200ft×200ft (2,500m×60m)
10/28 11,150ft×230ft (3,400m×70m)

Leningrad has come to be known by an increasing number of travellers from the West and as befits the massive scope of Soviet domestic airline operations, is a large airport with an imposing passenger terminal.

Located just 370 miles to the north-west of Moscow and 1,300 miles from London, the former capital of Russia is a principal hub for the operations of Aeroflot, the state airline. Located on the 'European side' of the USSR, Leningrad is also the gateway to the West, and frequent services are operated from here to European and Scandinavian capitals.

The terminal facilities at Leningrad have undergone various stages of modernisation in the past few years, to a degree whereby the lounges are comfortable and the check-in and other facilities bear strong comparison with many other European airports. A recent development took place in 1973, when new terminal halls were built, and a number of new facilities introduced, such as a loung for mothers with small children. Leningrad's new terminal hall was proudly proclaimed at this date as being 'larger than a football pitch'. The terminal structure itself is of striking design, with five centrally-disposed glass towers, which give natural illumination to the cavernous hall.

Leningrad Airport is one of the important airports on the massive Soviet air transport network.

Lisbon International

Portugal

Location: 4 miles from Lisbon city centre
Elevation: 374ft (114m)
Runways in use: 2
18/36 7,872ft×150ft (2,400m×45m)
03/21 12,480ft×150ft (3,803m×45m)
Airport area: 1,275 acres
Passengers handled in 1981: 2,940,687
Total air transport movements 1981: 37,954
Cargo handled in 1981: 46,200 tonnes

From the small country of Portugal, navigators headed out across the world first with their sailing ships to colonise lands in distant parts and stamp on them the indelible Portuguese mark. In South America in the west, in India, Africa, and Timor in the east, sions of the far-ranging nature of missionaries from Imperial Portugal remain strong today, even though the country no longer has any strong overseas political power. Aviation came later, when in 1922 two Portuguese aviators, Coutinho and

Cabral, made the first aerial crossing of the South Atlantic. Lisbon Airport was opened for business 20 years after that occasion, on 1 December 1942, when most of the western world was at war. For neutral Portugal this was a particularly significant occasion.

In its original form Lisbon Airport had a passenger terminal and four runways, the longest of which was 3,900ft and which were excellent for their time. In those first years, when traffic was reduced to a shadow of what it could have been because of the war, the airport nevertheless became a scheduled stopping place for almost a dozen airlines, and established Lisbon as a modern air terminal for international flights.

From the postwar period traffic steadily increased up to the point where 2.5 million passengers were being handled in 1970 and a total of 43,000 aircraft movements were being recorded annually, with consequent additions to the number of terminal facilities.

73

In concert with the increasing traffic, alterations have been made to the airport since the start of the jet age and up to the present time, when various plans have been drawn for a completely new airport to serve the country's capital city. The economic climate in Portugal has restrained the construction of a brand new airport, however, and for the moment developments continue at the present site.

Lisbon International is a comfortable and well-sited airport, located near the coast and just 20 minutes drive (four miles) from the city centre. The style of the terminal buildings is dated by today's standards, but the interior of the passenger halls has been steadily modernised to answer today's needs. Thirty years of operation have also been enough to establish orange and other trees which impart a friendly atmosphere at the airport.

Lisbon Airport today has two runways, the longest of which is 12,500ft, and they see 38,000 air transport aircraft movements annually. The airport is served by 88 scheduled airlines and numerous non-scheduled carriers, with the bulk of this traffic being handled by the national carrier Transportes Aéreos Portugueses (TAP). In 1976 TAP was responsible for 68.3% of the passenger traffic handled at Lisbon, and accounted for 51.9% of air transport movements. In that year there was an average of 687 scheduled and non-scheduled commercial flights every week, with a maximum of 683 movements in one peak summer week.

A new airport has been projected for Lisbon for some years but the existing airport continues to be the main hub for traffic.

Ten types of aircraft were using Lisbon Airport in 1976, with the Boeing 727 heading the list with the greatest number of movements — 40.3%. The Boeing 707 was the second busiest type at Lisbon (30%) thus illustrating a measure of the airport's noise problem, for the quieter B747 and DC-10 were at that date still only accounting for 9.3% of total movements between them. Unfortunately, Lisbon Airport creates a noise problem, which the authorities have been working hard to minimise. The number of night flights allowed has been steadily reduced, and the take-offs have been re-routed to reduce the number of movements overflying the city from 4.044 to 3,434 in 1976. This position has since improved further and will continue to improve as the noisier aircraft are phased out. Ultimately, however, a new airport for Lisbon may be the only answer to this thorny problem.

The matter of a new international airport for Lisbon has been the subject of discussion for well over a decade, but the funding for this major project remains a problem. Equally, no decision has been taken over the proposed site. It is likely that, initially, at least, development of the present airport will be carried out, to provide for a maximum passenger throughput of seven million passengers annually.

London (Heathrow)   UK

Location: 15 miles west of London
Elevation: 80ft (24m)
Runways in use: 3
10L/28R 12,800ft×150ft (3,900m×46m)
05R/23L 7,734×150ft (2,350m×46m)
10R/28L 11,972ft×150ft (3,650m×46m)
Airport area: 2,719 acres
Passengers handled in 1981: 26,400,800
Total aircraft movements in 1981: 247,100
Cargo handled in 1981: 450,400 tonnes

Few airports have come in for so much criticism, controversy and discussion in the press at Heathrow Airport, while at the same time handling such a large traffic and acting as a highly efficient terminal point for world-ranging airliners.

Heathrow Airport is unique in being the busiest International airport in the world, in the amount of money that is spent there annually, and in its style, which has made expanding civil air operations difficult from the outset. It is continually under fire from local residents because of the noise that it generates, and from operators because its landing fees for airliners are among the highest in the world. For the travelling public it has been called 'the world's most hated airport', while airline pilots have nothing but praise for the efficiency of the air traffic control.

Heathrow was first planned as an aerodrome in 1943 when World War II was at its height. It was clear that the Royal Air Force Transport Command would need an aerodrome for the operation of

trooping flights to the Far East, and some 50 sites were examined for this purpose. The one considered to be most suitable was near Feltham in Middlesex, situated between Hounslow and Staines. There was an aerodrome already there at the time, used by the Fairey Aviation Company and known as Heathrow. This aerodrome was, in fact, not far from the original site at Hounslow Heath from where the first international civil aviation services began on 25 August 1919.

Work began on the new RAF aerodrome in 1944, but the war against Japan ended before it reached a very advanced stage, and because of its proximity to London it was subsequently decided to make this a civil airport for the capital. When it was approved that this should be the main London Airport, administration passed from the Royal Air Force to the then Ministry of Civil Aviation.

Limited operations were possible in 1946, and the first airliner to take off from the new airport was British South American Airways' Avro Lancastrian *Star Light*, which left London Airport on 1 January 1946 on a proving flight to Buenos Aires. BSAA opened a regular service on this route in March 1946. On 1 May 1946, Heathrow was officially opened to air traffic, by which time it had been named officially London Airport.

Within a few years it was clear that much work

While the talk of a fifth terminal for Heathrow continues, the Terminal 4 plan, on the south side of the airport, is being brought to fruition.

would have to be done to bring the airport up to standard if London was to have an international airport suitable for the capital, and the first of a long line of expansion programmes was begun. A new 120ft control tower was built, together with a large passenger building (now known as Terminal 2) and an administration and crew rest block, later called Queen's Building. The first of these buildings was opened for use on 17 April 1955. This area was officially named London Airport Central.

The next development scheme to be put in hand was that devised by the Millbourn Committee, which had been drawn up in the late 1950s to examine ways in which London Airport could best be expanded and utilised in the future. It was already clear that the central terminal island arrangement was confining and offered little possibility for expansion. Amongst other things, the Committee found that the best way of making the most of what they had with London Airport was to withdraw one runway from the original six planned and then withdraw a second runway from use to provide more space for building. It was also recommended that a pier system between the buildings and apron be constructed, that a long-haul passenger terminal be erected, and a second short-haul passenger building constructed on the north-east face.

The new long-haul passenger building, later called Terminal 3, was opened first in November 1961, at which point the original Terminal 1 was joined with the terminal used for European flights, and in this united form became known as Terminal 2. The new terminal planned to the north-east came into use in 1969, and was then designated Terminal 1. This terminal used by British Airways for domestic and European flights and subsequently by one or two European carriers, gave the airport its third passenger terminal, and this is the situation up to the present day.

Subsequent to this work the new cargo terminal, colloquially known as Cargo Village, was built to provide air freight facilities for carriers using the airport, and which included numerous all-cargo airlines. In its initial form this terminal area covered 165 acres and cost £20 million.

On the terminal front, further work was done in the early 1970s on Terminal 3 and, adjacent to this, a new long-haul international arrivals section was built. Air jetties were installed at the growing number of passenger piers in the central area, and the number of multi-storey car parks increased. Such developments have brought us up to the present time, when it is acknowledged that the airport is as good as saturated by passenger traffic in the peak periods of a year, and when the limit of terminal expansion has almost been reached.

Various additional measures are being taken wherever possible to provide for the ever rising tide of travellers passing through Heathrow, numbers that now make London Airport the fourth busiest in the world. Amongst these measures has been the creation of a new, £7 million terminal satellite built on the airside face of the Queen's Building. It is linked with Terminals 1 and 2 and equipped with moving walkways.

Another development has been the completion of an underground rail link from Hounslow West to the centre of the airport, which makes it possible for passengers to travel from the West End of London right into the heart of the airport by the one underground train. This underground rail link does offer a valuable service for travellers, and compensates to some degree for the withdrawal of check-in facilities at the old West London Air Terminal.

The new rail link offers no relief to the British Airport Authority providing crucially needed terminal space, however, and a fourth terminal is now a feature of the Authority's plans. To be located on the south side of the airport, Terminal 4 is intended to raise the capacity of the airport to 38 million passengers/year. This capacity is expected to be the ultimate for Heathrow, and may be reached by 1990. Terminal 4 is scheduled to enter service in 1985. Improvements have also recently been made to Terminals 2 and 3, and a £5.5 million improvement programme to Terminal 1 was completed in January 1982. More long-term car parking space has been added (raising these spaces to 6,314), and a £3 million baggage improvement scheme was started in March 1982. — Most importantly, landing fees were frozen until April 1983.

Busiest passenger airport in Europe and busiest international airport in the world, London Heathrow is now neat and tidy in spite of the construction work that seems always in train.

Los Angeles International   USA

Location: 20 miles from Los Angeles city centre
Elevation: 126ft (38m)
Runways in use: 5
25L/07R 12,000ft×200ft (3,657m×60m)
25R/07L 12,090ft×150ft (3,684m×45m)
24L/06R 10,285ft×150ft (3,135m×45m)
24R/06L 8,925ft×150ft (2,720m×45m)
26/08 3,000ft×75ft (914m×23m) general aviation; daylight hours and VFR only)
Airport area: 3,500 acres
Passengers handled in 1981: 32,722,500
Total air transport movements in 1981: 380,200
Cargo handled in 1981: 697,700 tons

Apart from being the third busiest airport in the world in terms of passenger traffic handled, LAX as the airport is otherwise known, is noteworthy in being based on the satellite concept of design, in which individual passenger terminals are reached by tunnels from the central area. This involved the placing around the central section of satellite buildings served directly by the aircraft taxiing in from the adjoining pairs of parallel runways. The system thus decentralises traffic while at the same time gives as much freedom to aircraft as possible, and eliminates congestion of the central area. This is given over to car parks (there is space for a total of 18,000 cars), the main restaurants and the airport's control tower and administration building.

In 1926 the city of Los Angeles first considered establishing a municipal airport near Inglewood and in 1927 a group of local citizens chose 640 acres of a ranch area for the airport site. In 1928 one Clifford Henderson was appointed the first director of the 'airport', which in fact, comprised a dirt strip for the runway and no buildings and was called Mines Field.

In the same year the city of Los Angeles leased the present site of the airport for 50 years for a rent of $124,800 a year. Two 100ft hangars were built on the south side of the airport at a cost of $35,000 each. On 7 June 1930 the airport was officially opened, and in 1930 the famous Douglas Aircraft Company began operations operations at the airport. Four years later Douglas wasjoined by the North American Aviation Company, which erected a plant at the airport with 90,000sq ft of floor space.

The postwar years saw the big development of the airport, and in 1949 the airport was officially renamed Los Angeles International. In December 1957 ground-breaking was begun for the start of a jet age terminal and other improvements, the terminal being dedicated by the then vice-president, Lyndon B. Johnson, in June 1962, with the dedication of the International Carriers Satellite, the new jet age terminal complex became fully operational.

The $100 million terminal at LAX was built under the administration of the Board of Airport Commissioners and the Los Angeles Department of Airports, and occupies 265 acres of the 3,500-acre airport site. The terminal is made up of the individual-ticketing and satellite units, which are constructed in two levels. There are 13 ticketing-satellite buildings, which are two storeys high with provision for a third storey when required. The first floor, on the parking level, is given over to ticketing and baggage facilities. The second floor is for

Los Angeles International is third busiest in the world. 'Theme Building', with suspended restaurant, is behind control tower.

administrative use. The ticketing buildings are connected to their individual satellites by underground channels, some 400ft long and 20ft wide, which enable passengers to reach the aircraft manoeuvring areas without being in the way of the aircraft and many vehicles operating on the surface. This routing also directs passengers to particular parts of the airport for specific flights. Each satellite, built on the apron level, is able to service 12 jet aircraft simultaneously. With most airlines at LAX passengers board the aircraft by way of airbridges, which means the passengers never usually set foot on the apron. the satellite terminals contain lobby areas, restaurants, news-stands and other public rooms.

The two northerly terminals, which adjoin parallel runways 06L and 06R, are used by international carriers, while the satellite terminals to the south are used by US carriers. To the west of the central area is a commuter terminal, used by air taxi aircraft and commercial helicopters as well as third-level operators.

Los Angeles International runs down to the Pacific Ocean, and is separated from the sea by only a small

International carrier satellite terminal is pictured in foreground, with US airline terminals seen at rear.

housing estate and the Vista Del Mar, a seafront drive. Overlooking the airports and the twin pairs of runways, is the 172ft high control tower building. Next to this impressive building it the Theme Building, which is in fact a restaurant building constructed in parabolic arches which soar 135ft above the ground. The airport authorities say that this Theme Building symbolises the futuristic character of the airport, and they have placed the restaurant among the arches 70ft above the ground; it will accommodate 300 diners, who have an all round view of the airport's activities from this lofty perch.

With its first 50 years of operation behind it, Los Angeles International is considering the possibility of 40 million passengers a year using the airport by 1984. Further developments, such as improving access roads and additional terminal improvements, will be required, and plans are already being studied to this end.

Madrid (Barajas) Spain

Location: 7 miles ENE of city
Elevation: 1,998ft (607m)
Runways in use: 2
01/19 12,139ft×150ft (3,700m×45m)
15/33 13,451ft×150ft (4,100m×45m)
Passengers handled in 1981: 9,960,000
Total aircraft movements in 1981: 114,400
Cargo handled in 1981: 151,000 tonnes

Madrid's original airport was located at Getafe with a single runway. This came into use during the 1920s and is still used, but in the 1930s a new airport was built at Barajas, on the present site. This was to become the site for the main airport at Madrid and, indeed, Spain, and with its present annual traffic of over 10 million passengers, Madrid is a very busy

European airport, seeing more terminal passengers in 1980 than Amsterdam Schiphol and the UK's Gatwick (the number of international passengers handled by Schiphol was over twice that of Madrid Barajas, however).

A major redevelopment plan was drawn up for Barajas in 1949, and this development work continued right through the 1950s to produce a multi-runway arrangement and a sizeable terminal complex. An international terminal was built in 1972 adjoining the earlier terminal. This was opened in 1974 and equipped six boarding concourses with air bridges.

It is considered that Barajas Airport could handle traffic for Madrid up to the year 2000, but because of the growth in the traffic in recent times the Spanish

Ministry of Transport and Communications is planning a completely new airport for the capital. The location is known but is not being publicised for the time being to avoid land speculation, which has occurred with other Spanish airport development work in the past.

Meanwhile, an improvement programme at Barajas has been newly instituted, and the first stage of this programme was begun in July 1981. This phase involved complete modernisation of the national terminal, to accelerate baggage handling and eliminate delays. To ease traffic congestion between the airport and the city centre a new highway, the M40 is planned, and other road improvements are being studied.

The striking Spanish landscape surrounding Madrid Airport is shown dramatically here, with the equally eye-catching runway arrangement.

Manchester (Ringway)   UK

Location: 7.5 miles SSW of Manchester
Elevation: 256ft (75m)
Runways in use: 2
06/24 10,000ft × 150ft (3,030m × 45m)
Airport area: 1,342 acres
Passengers handled in 1981: 4,875,164
Total aircraft movements in 1981: 60,900
Cargo handled in 1981: 28,800 tonnes

The first site for Manchester Airport was at Wythenshawe, selected in 1929. Within a year, however, this site was replaced by an airport at Barton 1930, and some £51,000 was spent on the development of that airport. The Barton site remained Manchester's airport until the search began in 1934 for a better location. This was found at Ringway, just a few miles from Wythenshawe, and on 25 June 1938 Manchester (Ringway) Airport was opened officially, by HM Secretary of State for Air, Sir Kingsley Wood.

The first aircraft to use the airport was a Douglas DC-2 belonging to KLM, which actually flew into Ringway on 24 June 1938. The airport at that time consisted largely of a prepared grass landing area, and covered some 250 acres. Subsequently Manchester Corporation purchased a total 660 acres to permit further development. Additional ground has been purchased since to bring the airport to its present size. The airport was impressed into service for the RAF when the war came, and the first runways were laid.

Postwar operation of the airport was finally vested in Manchester Corporation in 1953, when the Corporation settled with the Ministry of Aviation the airport's ownership and management. Five years later Manchester Corporation embarked on a large scale improvement plan for the airport, a prime feature of which was a fine new control tower and terminal building. This was opened by HRH the Duke of Edinburgh on 22 October 1962.

Another feature of this development scheme was the creation of two piers, one for domestic and one for international flights, the longer of which stretched for 970ft across the apron. By 1968 the airport was handling two million passengers/year. Another feature was the installation of a hydrant fuel system,

which eliminated the need for large numbers of tankers moving about the apron to refuel aircraft.

In 1973 further development work was put in hand to fit the airport for Jumbo jets and to raise its capacity to seven million passengers annually by 1982. This programme involved the doubling of the capacity of the control tower administration block for operational purposes; the erection of an additional long-haul pier, to be equipped with airbridges, the construction of a 13-level carpark, the enlargement of the international departure and transit lounge, the provision of a new Immigration and Customs hall, and the extension of the whole southern airside frontage at first and second floor levels. A number of other works were included.

The new pier can accept in the nose-in position four wide-bodied aircraft and three narrow, or seven B707 types. The original international pier is regularly occupied by 14 large aircraft. There are also six new remote aircraft stands.

A new purpose-built cargo terminal is planned for 1985, to increase the airport's capacity to 250,000 tonnes a year.

A second passenger terminal will be built by 1988, and a rail link to the airport is proposed.

Recent policy at Manchester has been to turn the airport into an important international hub for the UK. One development has been the construction of the direct link to the terminal from the M56 motorway.

Manila International

Philippines

Location: 5 miles SE of city
Elevation: 74ft (23m)
Runways in use: 2
06/24 11,000ft×200ft (3,350m×60m)
13/31 7,956ft×100ft (2,425m×30m)
Passengers handled in 1978: 4,000,400
Total aircraft movements in 1978: 57,000
Cargo handled in 1978: 26,600 tonnes

In the 1930s Manila was served by a small airport called Neilson, and this was equipped with only relatively short strips, 870m long. This was succeeded after World War 2 by Makati Airport, until the present site was developed. As the main international airport for the Philippines, Manila International saw a steady increase in tourist traffic as the Pacific war faded into a memory, leading to the need for a completely new airport; this brand new airport was opened for services at the beginning of 1982. Costing some Pesos 800 million — about £55 million — the new passenger terminal features a Y-shaped main building, with two satellites connected by a concourse. There are separate levels for arrivals and departures, and the handling capability is some 1,750 passengers an hour, or 4.3 million a year. There are 52 check-in counters with separate first-class and tourist-class desks. There is an extensive duty-free shopping arcade, separate VIP lounges and spacious arrival and departure halls.

The new facility is designed to handle traffic up to 1992 at least, at which point passenger throughput is expected to be running at some eight million passengers a year for the whole airport. A further plan for development beyond the year 2000 is then expected to be implemented.

The design for the new international passenger terminal at Manila Airport shows the use of airbridges throughout.

Melbourne

Australia

Location: 12 miles NW of Melbourne
Elevation: 402ft (122m)
Runways in use: 2
16/34 12,005ft×150ft (3,660m×45m)
09/27 7,500ft×150ft (2,287m×45m)
Airport area: 6,000 acres
Passengers handled in 1981: 6,144,781
Total aircraft movements in 1981: 81,931
Cargo handled in 1981: 98,180 tonnes

The provision of major international air terminals on the great continent of Australia is paramount to a country which is the biggest island in the world. Sydney and Melbourne have both had airports since 1921, with the present Sydney Airport located in substantially the same place, nine miles from the city centre, as when it began services to civil aviation. Melbourne Airport has had several locations however, varying in the last 58 years from 4-12 miles from the city centre.

In 1958 the Australian Department of Civil Aviation convened a panel to consider the possibilities of a future airport for Melbourne. After due deliberation, the panel recommended the development of the Tullamarine area, while at the same time pronouncing that no further extension could be made to the existing airport, at Essendon. Examination of the airspace requirements for the area finally determined that Tullamarine should be the site developed, and Australian Government approval was obtained in 1959 to acquire the necessary 5,300 acres of land required for the planned airport.

The airport was introduced into service on a phased basis from 1970, when terminal facilities for international operations were completed first. Domestic terminal facilities were introduced gradually from 1971, and the transfer of major operators from Essendon to the new Melbourne Airport was made from that time.

Situated on an area of gently sloping land 400ft above sea level, Melbourne Airport is bounded to the east and west by deep valleys. The soil is a clay type, but drainage conditions are excellent. There is ample space for future expansion, and duplication of the runway system if necessary. A freeway was constructed by the State Roads Authority, and links the airport and its approaches to the centre of Melbourne. An internal road system connects various areas of the airport with each other and to the external roads. An elevated roadway runs along the face of the terminal building at first floor level, and provides access to the terminal for departing passengers arriving by airport bus or taxi. There is a seven-acre landscaped car park fronting the terminal building accommodating 1,200 cars. With other car parks, to the north, south and east, there is room in the terminal area for over 6,000 cars.

Melbourne Airport is now handling over six million passengers a year. The airport is built on a plateau, 400ft above sea level.

The terminal complex design comprises an angular terminal with three sections, the central section being the longest. Facing a wide apron, each of the three terminal sections is equipped with a pier, or loading concourse. The central pier is an enclosed structure of two storeys, 570ft long and terminating in a Y with two sub piers at its end. This constitutes the international loading concourse. The north and south concourses, stretching as straight piers across the apron, are used primarily for domestic operations, depending upon traffic flow at Melbourne. The design is straightfoward and uncluttered, and accommodates all the usual facilities required for the handling and clearance of arriving and departing passengers. At each aircraft parking position there is a holding lounge for passengers, who board their aircraft by way of airbridges from the upper level of the two storeys in each pier; the apron level is given over to mechanical services, baggage handling and airline duties.

An initial two runways were laid down, and the pavements of these constructed to accept aircraft of up to 800,000lb weight. The runways are to standard ICAO specification as to width, that is 150ft with 25ft paved shoulders, and are generally flexible, with 58in to 64in thicknesses. Because the runways were built virtually parallel to those at the Essendon Airport, they are operated within the same air traffic control pattern. The runways incorporate high speed turnoffs, which enable aircraft to leave the runways at speeds of up to 60mph, and which as a result clears the runways more swiftly for following aircraft, thereby increasing the airport's handling capacity, particularly at peak periods.

The airport now has an Exposition Centre, and a 240-bed airport motel, a facility unique to Australia. 17 scheduled airlines serve the airport.

Mexico City DF (Benito Juarez)   Mexico

Location: 3 miles east of city
Elevation: 7,341ft (2,237m)
Runways in use: 3
05L/23R 10,170ft×130ft (3,100m×40m)
05R/23L 13,196ft×150ft (4,022m×45m)
13/31 7,546ft×131ft (2,300m×40m)
Airport area: 2,200 acres
Passengers handled in 1978: 9,428,505
Total aircraft movements in 1978: 207,000
Cargo handled in 1978: 215,000 tons

Mexico City International Airport has one of the highest elevations in the world, and it is not surprising therefore that a 13,000ft long runway is provided for the aircraft. First commercial flights at Mexico City actually used a military aerodrome at Belbuena, but the Mexico Central Airport was opened in 1929 on the present site. The runway complex has been changed over the years — the original 800m long strip running north to south, being realigned before the war, and then further runway arrangement work was done in the postwar years. One of the runways was later withdrawn from use, and the present arrangement provides for two main runways, bisected by a third.

The changes to the runways have meant a frequent redesign of the apron area, and the passenger terminal has also undergone reshaping and rearrangement. A completely new international airport has been considered for Mexico City with construction of this planned north-east of the city, but it seems now to have been decided that another runway will be built at Benito Juarez instead, and this runway will increase the handling capacity of the present airport from 60 movements an hour to about 96 movements per peak hour. In the past, aircraft movements have doubled every four years.

Miami International   USA

Location: 4 miles from city centre
Elevation: 10ft (3m)
Runways in use: 3
9R/27L 13,000ft×150ft (3,940m×45m)
9L/27R 10,500ft×200ft (3,182m×61m)
12/30 9,600ft×150ft (2,910m×45m)
Airport area: 3,000 acres
Passengers handled in 1981: 12,780,300
Total aircraft movements in 1981: 132,600
Cargo handled in 1981: 132,000 tonnes

The roots of aviation history at Miami can be traced to the Miami Country Club golf course, located a few short miles east of the present Miami International Airport. On 21 July 1911, a crowd estimated at 5,000 saw Miami's first aeroplane flight, which took place from that site. The event was a feature of the city's 15th birthday celebrations.

Operators considered Miami for a long time after that as a likely place for locating a flying base, and the enlightened Mayor Sewell, who had been largely responsible for the 1911 event, had written to the Wright brothers asking them to establish a flying school in Miami. The City even offered a $1,000 bonus fee as an attraction, but the Wright brothers turned down the offer. But aviation pioneer Glen Curtiss undertook to run a flying school in Miami during the winter months, and a 200ft×800ft long landing strip was prepared for the purpose.

Then in 1917 the US Navy created one of the most efficient training fields used in World War 1 at Dinner Key, and some 25 training aeroplanes were in the air for most of the daylight hours at the site.

In 1923 Capt Eddie Rickenbacker, World War 1 fighter ace and pioneer operator of Eastern Air Lines, found in Miami the ideal spot for his airline operations. Rickenbacker set up Florida Airways and ran that for a few years from 1923. In 1928 Pan American Airways made a clearing amidst the scrub and brushwood and created the 116-acre 'Pan American Field', and this field, just a few miles from the city, became the base that was eventually to be turned into Miami International Airport.

Pan American Field was designated as the third airport of entry in the USA, and on 15 September 1928 a Pan American Sikorsky S-38 amphibian rolled to the end of the dirt runway and took-off south towards Key West, where mail and passengers would be transferred to a larger Fokker F.10 for the flight to Havana. This was the first scheduled flight from what is now Miami International Airport.

By the late 1930s there were five airlines operating from Miami, including Pan American and Eastern Air Lines. National Airlines was then established at Miami, and the Pan American Field was the centre of commercial aviation in the area.

After World War 2 the Dade Board of County Commissioners began negotiations to purchase Pan American Field with a view to development of the airport into a major facility. In 1949 the Seaboard railroad tracks bisecting the airport were removed, and the army airport on the south side and the passenger airport on the north side were joined. With various land purchases and annexations the total acreage was raised to some 2,800, and the whole complex was given a name, Miami International Airport.

From 1951 an intense period of development followed. A new terminal building was constructed, and a 270-room hotel was erected. Eastern Air Lines built a $6 million hangar and maintenance complex, and National Airlines completed the construction of maintenance hangars and office buildings, and Delta Air Lines spent $2 million on a maintenance centre. With the first scheduled jet passenger flight in the United States taking place from Miami International (to New York, by National Airlines) on 10 December 1958, MIA entered the jet age. Further jet-related developments followed.

Miami International today is a massive facility

which is served by 81 scheduled airlines, said to be the most at any US airport. The airport is ranked second in the United States in terms of international passengers and also second in international cargo tonnage handled. The airport has been ranked tenth in the world in total passengers handled and fifth in the world in cargo tonnage. Foreign visitors entering Florida through MIA in 1981 spent over $3 billion, and with the great emphasis on tourism in recent years, international arrivals through Miami International have been growing at 20% per year. From Miami International Airport in 1981, 1,786 departures were made each week on 24 airlines to 42 cities in the US and Canada, and 68 departures a week by nine airlines to 11 cities in Europe. Additionally, from Miami 135 departures a week by 16 airlines were made to eight Central American cities and 263 flights a week by 23 airlines to 25 South American cities. Similarly impressive numbers were operated to Mexico and the Bahamas and Caribbean.

The 'people-mover' rapid transit cars are a feature in Miami International, running around the airport to different buildings including the Customs and Immigration Building, at rear.

The scrub land of Miami has long ago disappeared to be replaced by the grand structures of MIA, and whose principal feature today is the semi-circular terminal building with its seven piers and related concourses dispersed widely over the apron. Parking stands around these piers already offer, or shortly will offer, positions for well over 100 aircraft, and with a further development plan in hand, designed to take the airport to the year 2000, additional piers, satellite terminals and remoted locations will provide parking places for well over 56 more aircraft.

The development of the original terminal facility is perhaps one of the most distinctive characteristics of Miami International, for the early buildings have been reshaped and reconstructed and expanded to a remarkable degree, and almost beyond recognition, and yet further work in this direction is in hand. A number of international satellite terminals have already been started or planned, and one of these has been operating since January 1977, the 12-gate mid-field satellite terminal. By 1985 there will be at least one more of these satellite terminals operating and by the year 2000 perhaps half a dozen. The first satellite cost $15 million, and is located a quarter of

Miami International is in the middle of an expansion programme, with this being Phase One of the cargo terminal development.

a mile west of the main terminal. It is a four-storey building with a transit lounge.

Connection to the Customs and immigration building and the main terminal is made by way of an electric Satellite Transit Shuttle, which carries people at 20mph in two electric trams over the quarter of a mile, one-minute journey. Each tram of the SS has three 50-passenger cars. The electric Shuttle' system was introduced in April 1980, before which buses were used to carry passengers to and from the terminals.

The satellite terminal has 12 aircraft positions with passenger loading bridges adjustable to various aircraft heights. Modular construction allows for expansion of the building to 18 gates; seating capacity on both levels is 1,100 people, and the building has been designed to handle six million passengers a year.

In an age when security considerations have been responsible for the closure of many observation decks, the international satellite terminal at Miami has been provided with a sun deck, which enables passengers waiting for a flight to gain spectacular views of the aircraft operations at the airport.

Miami International is operated by the Aviation Department of Metropolitan Dade County, which is a quasi-autonomous authority of the city of Miami.

Milan (Malpensa/Linate)   Italy

MALPENSA
Location: 30 miles NW of Milan in the Province of Varese
Elevation: 767ft (234m)
Runways in use: 2
17L/35R 12,844ft×200ft (3,915m×60m)
17R/35L 8,620ft×200ft (2,268m×60m)
Passengers handled in 1980: 1,166,459
Total aircraft movements in 1980: 14,180
Cargo handled in 1980: 45,739 tonnes

LINATE
Location: 4 miles east of Milan
Elevation: 352ft (108m)
Runways in use: 2
18/36 7,337ft×200ft (2,236m60m)
1,968ft×72ft (600m×22m) (general aviation)
Passengers handled in 1980: 5,397,613
Total aircraft movements in 1980: 82,620
Cargo handled in 1980: 50,027 tonnes

Milan has two airports, Malpensa and Linate, of which Linate is the older in terms of international air traffic, but Malpensa is the larger.

Both airports have a history which dates back to the early 1900s. For the Italian aeronatutical engineer Gianni Caproni established a base at Linate for his aircraft work in about 1930, while the famous Italian designer Giovanni Agusta had associations with Malpensa from as early as 1907. In 1924 an airport was built at Malpensa, and used by the

military in later years, and at Linate the first civil airport was built in 1930 when the site was named Aeroporto Enrico Forlanini, in memory of the Italian aeronautical pioneer.

Both airports were used after the war for commercial traffic and Malpensa was turned into an airport for larger aircraft in November 1948 when modernisation was begun. Linate underwent a similar facelift in 1958-62. By now, however, a new airport service company, created for the development and management of both airports had been brought into being, and this company, Societa Esercizi Aeroportuali, otherwise known as SEA, was created as an autonomous association with 84.5% of the share capital held by the Milan Municipality and 14.5% by Milan Province.

SEA decreed that both airports be modernised and that Linate initially be assigned to domestic traffic only, with Malpensa becoming the intercontinental airport. In 1972 the Italian Ministry of Transport approved a new master plan for Malpensa which will extend its traffic handling capability up to the year 2000. Milan-Malpensa is the airport on which prime work is being concentrated. The master plan provides for a passenger terminal with a potential for handling up to 12 million passengers a year, at a throughflow rate of 7,500 passengers an hour. The building will have seven floors and a depth towards the apron of about 300ft. There will be two satellites, and parking space on the air side for about 20 aircraft in the nose-position. These aircraft will be reached by the air bridges. Other aircraft, parked in remoter positions, will be served by apron buses.

The master plan for development of Malpensa provides also for a new air freight terminal, a bonded warehouse, Customs building, buildings for airline operators, airport personnel and large car parks. Work on the development of both airports is now well in hand, and the programme for Linate was scheduled to be completed in 1982, and that for Malpensa in 1983. Linate will present to the public greatly amplified arrivals and departure halls, for both domestic and international passengers.

Milan-Malpensa has a history dating back to the early 1900s. Passenger check-in is in process here, with a blissfully-short queue.

Milan-Linate Airport has undergone major re-working recently, as shown here. Both Linate and Milan-Malpensa are managed by the organisation SEA.

Montreal (Mirabel)

Canada

Location: 34 miles NW of city
Elevation: 257ft (78m)
Runways in use: 2
11L-29R 12,045ft×200ft (3,650m×61m)
06RC/24LC 12,045ft×200ft (3,650m×61m)
Airport area: Total operational area 17,290 acres
Passengers handled in 1981: 1,401,400
Air transport movements in 1981: 32,800

In the early 1970s when Dorval Airport was the principal traffic hub for Montreal, the dangers of saturation were recognised, and a study made concluded that even with enlargement Dorval did not have a future beyond 1985 as the main airport for the city, because by then it would be quite unable to handle the traffic. Consequently, a new airport for the city was planned, and Montreal Mirabel was opened for traffic on 29 November 1975.

The site chosen for Montreal's new international airport did not, unfortunately, capture the interest of very many — except perhaps the construction companies — for while it was one of the best sites found by Transport Canada, the Canadian Department of Transportation, it was nevertheless a very long way from the city it was scheduled to serve, and travellers today have a one-hour bus drive between the city and the airport, which hardly tends to make Mirabel a conveniently-located city facility. This compares with Dorval Airport, which is about 15 miles from the city centre, and which had been a main airport for the city since 1941. While there are

now 36 airlines serving Montreal Mirabel, the airlines have been very slow to move to the facility, and even today Dorval is handling six times the traffic of Mirabel, or 6,226,000 passengers in 1981, this an increase of 1% over the year before; by comparison Mirabel's passenger traffic actually declined by 9.7% in 1981.

Mirabel nevertheless is a modern and fine airport, and offers the great asset of capability for expansion for very many years to come. On the massive site in the Quebec countryside there are in fact some 89,000 acres available for the airport to 'grow into'. As of the moment, the airport's operational area in the phase one development stage covers 5,200 acres of the 17,000 acres that have been set aside for the operational zone.

In this operational area there is a massive angular terminal building, containing long lines of check-in counters and the usual airline offices, airy and spacious passenger waiting lounges, duty-free shops, restaurants and waiting areas, and the airline administration centres and services for travellers. The airport area also contains the two main runways which have a capacity for 300,000 aircraft

Montreal's newest airport of Mirabel was designed to take airport noise and traffic away from city dwellers, while still making the airport's services readily available for travellers. Thus, the airport is well in the countryside.

movements a year, while the main runway O6RC/24LC has been earmarked for possible extension to 4,575m, or no less than 15,100ft. The airport's control tower/air traffic control centre is perhaps the world's tallest, at 215ft (65m)

When Mirabel was being planned, Transport Canada elected to make the site one of the largest in the world, and as the airport is designed to serve the needs of Mirabel and Canada in the year 2000, it was probably felt that such a massive site might well be needed. The location of the airport was also influenced greatly by the matter of aircraft noise, which is always a subject for complaint. It was therefore felt that development of the airport would be possible without in any way disturbing the neighbouring metropolis. Mirabel is thus located at the foot of the Laurentian Hills, far from the city and near the farmland and wooded areas north-west of Montreal.

It is felt that Mirabel presents a long-range solution to the problem of air service for the large metropolis. In its first stage, Mirabel has taken over all international flights as well as some connecting flights between large urban centres in Canada. For the moment, flights to and from the USA and most domestic flights in Canada will continue to use Dorval, until phase two of Mirabel is implemented. In its eventual form, by the early years of the 21st century, Mirabel is expected to have a total of six runways and six terminals, a cargo centre and a satellite industrial and commercial zone.

In its Phase One development Mirabel has a passenger terminal and apron complex, a control and services area, an administration and commercial zone, with parking facilities, an air cargo complex, aircraft maintenance base and an animal quarantine area. There is a hotel, an aircraft sewage dumping station, an electrical substation, flight kitchens, a fuel farm, the control tower, fire/crash and rescue centre, and a taxi and bus centre.

Passengers board the aircraft at rectangular satellite terminals as well as the main building, and these satellites are called 'clusters'. Each cluster has six parking positions, so that 18 aircraft can be simultaneously handled. Passengers in transit join connecting flights by way of an Aeroquay and an underground passage through which they enter the terminal. At the moment, Mirabel is seeing some 33,000 air transport movements a year, or about a quarter of the movements currently at Dorval.

Because of the great amount of space available, great opportunity has been taken to introduce an air cargo zone, which will provide 1,200 acres of land for air cargo and related activities. The airport is being advertised, in fact, as a trans-shipment and air distribution centre for freight, with a view to many companies using it. A cargo warehouse with 600,000sq ft of space was built in 1976 for this purpose. There is no night curfew at the airport, and companies are able therefore to have freight moved through the airport 24 hours a day.

The cost of Mirabel Airport had reached Canadian $371 million by 1979, which included the total airport costs and land development costs. Air navigational service costs ran to another $6.6 million.

Moscow (Vnukovo/Sheremetievo)   USSR

VNUKOVO
Location: 17 miles SW of Moscow
Elevation: 669ft (204m)
Runways in use: 2
02/20 10,000ft×200ft (3,050m×60m)
06/24 9,840ft×260ft (3,000m×80m)

SHEREMETIEVO
Location: 17 miles NNW of Moscow
Elevation: 623ft (190m)
Runways in use: 1
07/25 11,480ft×260ft (3,500m×80m)
Passengers handled in 1980: 3,900,000

Moscow has four principal airports, Vnukovo, Sheremetievo, Bykovo and Domodedovo, of which Vnukovo was originally the main one. This was superseded by Sheremetievo in 1960 as the new major international airport for the capital, however, and Vnukovo has been relegated to handling shorter, domestic passenger flights. Of the others, Bykovo has been in existence for some years now and serves principally as cargo airport for the capital. The fourth of the quartet, Domodedovo, was opened for international passenger operations in 1966.

Vnukovo dates from pre-World War II days, when it had only a grass operational strip and a small terminal building. In postwar years it became the usual arrival airport for heads of state visiting the Soviet capital. A second airport terminal was constructed near the original one at Vnukovo, able to handle some 2,000 passengers an hour. While the airport has now given way to Sheremetievo as the international air gateway, it is still regarded as important to the Moscow airport system.

Domodedovo is one of the biggest airports in Europe, and while no information is available on the matter, it is almost certain that flights were made to the airport by the Tupolev Tu-144 supersonic airliner during the short period of operation of the world's only other supersonic transport.

The airport terminal building is 350yd long, interconnected with a control office, which oversees ramp services. The waiting hall covered a floor area of over 32,000sq ft. There is a balcony and roof garden in the building. On the outside, there are western style passenger piers, while on the landside there is parking space for over 1,000 cars.

Moscow's prime international airport, Sheremetievo, sees flights by all of the biggest and heaviest jets in international service. Sheremetievo is a good-looking airport, with no dramatic frills, but with spacious and well-lit terminal buildings, and the overall premises have a volume of some 5.3million cubic feet. The terminals have been handling traffic throughputs of 2,000 passengers an hour. The

Apron at Sheremetievo Airport, Moscow, one of the city's five airports.

airport is served by electric railway trains as well as bus services; there is also a heliport. The facilities at Sheremetievo were expanded for the 1980 Moscow Olympics.

Another development was the construction of a brand new airport, located 37 miles north-west of the centre of the capital and called Sheremetievo II. This new airport, otherwise known as Olympic Airport was built to handle traffic expected for the 22nd Olympic Games.

Olympic Airport was being built by the German company Rüterbau of Hanover, a subsidiary of the Salzgitter organisation, which won the contract for the project in May 1977 in competition with 30 well-known companies from all over the world. It cost some DM230 million and Rüterbau had a participating stake in the project of some DM35 million. The company was responsible for the

Striking terminal building at Sheremetievo Airport, which was built largely by the West German firm of Rüterbau.

replacement passenger terminal for Hanover Airport, and to which the Olympic Airport terminal bears a striking resemblance.

The design of Sheremetievo II Airport was based upon four prime requirements. To handle up to 2,100 passengers an hour in the peak period; to handle six million passengers a year; to serve simultaneously 19 aircraft of different types, and to cover no more than 915,000sq ft in terminal area. Negotiation of the contract between Rüterbau and the Soviet authorities occupied 18 months. With all requirements met, construction work began in July 1977. The construction work was done largely by German technicians and personnel, with prefabricated building sections being transported to Moscow from the Federal Republic of Germany.

The airport of Sheremetievo II is to be used exclusively for international flights, and should be a showcase in the Moscow airport system. There are two terminals integrated with a central administrative building, and two pairs of parallel runways. The building has 19 telescopic airbridges, and an initial handling capability for 31 aircraft. The Sheremetievo II terminal opened in 1980, and should handle up to six million passengers by 1990.

Nairboi (Jomo Kenyatta)   Kenya

Location: 7 miles ESE of city
Elevation: 5,307ft (1,618m)
Runways in use: 1
06/24 13,507ft × 150ft (4,117m × 45m)
Passengers handled in 1979: 1,451,588
Total aircraft movements in 1979: 19,468
Cargo handled in 1979: 29,000 tons

Formerly known as Embakasi, Jomo Kenyatta Airport
was given that name in December 1978 in honour of
the first President of Kenya who had died that year.
The airport replaces an earlier one called Nairobi
West, which had been in use until the time of World
War 2. Built near the Nairobi National Park Game
Reserve, Kenya's principal airport was offically
opened in March 1958. Subject to frequent
development programmes, covering the lengthening
of the runway and the building of a new terminal
complex, Nairobi's main airport has been at this site
ever since.

The terminal structure comprises a central arrivals
and administrative building encircled by a two-level
departure and transit building. Check-in facilities are
on the ground level, in two international units and a
domestic unit. Transit and departure lounges are on
the upper level with access to the aircraft by way of
air bridges.

In all, Jomo Kenyatta International is a good-
looking airport, located in an attractive part of the
world, and it is ·the destination for some 30
international airlines, including the flag-carrier,
Kenya Airways. In total, there are some 25 aircraft
stands, and there is a separate cargo terminal.

A new terminal was built in 1978, and a new
taxiway was introduced parallel to the western half
of the runway. Further development at Nairobi
International is expected to be made at the present
site.

New York (John F. Kennedy International)   USA

Location: 15 miles SE of Manhattan, New York
Elevation: 12ft (3.6m)
Runways in use: 5
04R/22L 8,400ft × 150ft (2,560m × 45m)
04L/22R 11,352ft × 150ft (3,460m × 45m)
13L/31R 10,000ft × 150ft (3,048m × 45m)
13R/31L 14,572ft × 150ft (4,440m × 45m)
14/32 2,560ft × 75ft (775m × 23m) (general aviation)
Airport area: 4,930 acres
Passengers handled in 1981: 25,752,700
Total aircraft movements in 1981: 228,000
Cargo handled in 1981: 1,191,500 tonnes

New York International Airport, known since
December 1963 as John F. Kennedy, is another of
the world's airports which has been built largely on
tracts of land reclaimed from the sea. The airport
was first planned in 1942, and its site was originally
occupied by a golf course and the waters of Jamaica
Bay, off New York City. The city filled in this site at a
cost of $60 million and leased it to the Port Authority
of New York and New Jersey. This lease has run
since June 1947, and saw the original dedication of
the airport on 31 July 1948. Commercial flights from
the airport actually began on 1 July 1948.

Initially, an airport of 1,100 acres was planned, or
one about twice the size of La Guardia, which was
becoming inadequate for both international and
domestic traffic. It was not envisaged that the airport
would eventually be nine times the size of La Guardia
and cover 4,930 acres, or an area equivalent to all of
Manhattan Island from 42nd Street to the Battery, at
the southern end of the Island.

In 1952 the PNYA completed an 11-storey
control tower, built 11 hangars and an air route
traffic control centre. In March 1955 construction
work began on a new central area of the airport
called Terminal City which covered 655 acres.
Features of this airport city were the international

Arrivals Building and two adjacent foreign flag wing
buildings, individual terminal buildings for US
airlines, a central heating and refrigeration plant, five
car parks, a 220-acre, landscaped international park,
7.5 miles of taxiways and 10 miles of two-lane
roads. The official dedication of the first part of
Terminal City took place on 5 December 1957, and
the Arrivals Building was opened on 6 December
1957.

Today, the central area consists of nine passenger
terminals surrounded by a dual ring of aircraft
taxiways. Originally 655 acres, this area was
enlarged to 840 acres. There is provision in the
central area for 6,600 cars, while in total there are
13,000 public car parking places at the airport.
Amongst the many facilities for travellers there is an
international hotel with 520 rooms, three car rental
buildings, a bus garage, and numerous shops,
observation decks and restaurants. The airport is
now handling almost 23 million passengers a year
and employs 41,000 people. To date the Port
Authority has invested some $702 million in the
airport.

A feature of John F. Kennedy International is the
arrangement whereby various airlines have erected
and operate their own passenger terminals, and thus
US flag carriers Pan American, Trans World Airlines,
Eastern Air Lines, United Airlines, American Airlines
and Northwest Airlines have their own individually
styled terminals, dramatic in design and efficient in
function. There is also a joint British Airways/Air
Canada terminal, while Lufthansa and Air France also
have terminal facilities of their own. At present there
are 145 aircraft gate positions serving the various
terminals. There are 13 US scheduled airlines serving
the airport, including the helicopter operator New
York Airways, 16 US and foreign charter airlines and
45 overseas airlines, making 74 airlines in total.

Air cargo has become so substantial at JFK that

Control tower and International Arrivals building at New York's John F. Kennedy Airport, once called Idlewild.

JFK Airport New York runs into the waters of Jamaica Bay, Queen's County, part of which was filled in to provide the airport site. The airport covers an area equivalent to the whole of New York's Manhattan Island.

the airport has developed into one of the most important air cargo centres in the world, and indeed is currently handling the greatest cargo tonnage amongst all the world's airports. In 1981 this was 1,191,500 tons. With 45 foreign airlines and 12 US cargo-carrying airlines using the airport, it became necessary to provide a special air cargo centre at JFK, and which is the largest in the United States. This occupies 344 acres and includes 23 cargo buildings, providing 2.5 million square feet. Not surprisingly, perhaps, with such a vast cargo throughput, large-scale theft problems were experienced at one stage. There are now 35 airfreight forwarders, Customs brokers and

Apart from being gateway airport to New York and eastern USA, JFK Airport is the world's No 1 cargo airport in terms of tonnage handled. Note over-wing passenger loading bridges serving B747s.

consolidator companies on the airport as well as numerous trucking firms and several Federal agencies.

There are two pairs of parallel runways at JFK while a fifth runway serves general aviation, private and business flying. The whole complex is overseen by the 150ft high control tower, which houses $1 million worth of air traffic control electronic equipment.

New York (La Guardia) USA

Location: 8 miles from Manhattan, New York
Elevation: 21ft (6m)
Runways in use: 3
04/22 7,000ft × 150ft (2,133m × 45m)
13/31 7,000ft × 150ft (2,133m × 45m)
14/32 2,000ft × 75ft (610m × 23m) (General Aviation)
Airport area: 650 acres
Passengers handled in 1981: 18,146,200
Total air transport movements in 1981: 215,000
Cargo handled in 1981: 36,800 tons

Known until the ascendancy of Kennedy International as 'New York's own', La Guardia Airport is named after the one-time mayor of New York City who was primarily instrumental in gaining its development as an airport to serve the business capital of the USA. Fiorello La Guardia achieved his

ambition of securing the airport for New York City in September 1937. Before that the one-time amusement park site had been used as a private flying field from 1929, when it was first named Glenn H. Curtiss Airport, and then North Beach Airport.

The airport was opened to commercial traffic on 2 December 1939 when the original site, covering 105 acres, was enlarged by the City's filling in of the waterfront on the airport east side. The airport grew into a 558-acre tract and then to cover 630 acres. It has been enlarged further in the last decade, and now covers 650 acres overall. It grew also to have three active runways and a large and elegant terminal complex fronted by a car park which was once a boat basin.

Today, New York's own airport continues to handle 18 million passengers/year and employ almost 9,000 people.

Operated by the Port Authority of New York and New Jersey, La Guardia plays a central role in the New York airport system as a largely domestic airport channelling passengers between New York City and the nation's west and south. In this task it is an important complementary airport to John F. Kennedy, which airport is now the principal hub for New York.

An expansion programme for the airport was begun in 1958, and then in 1964 a new central

While Kennedy Airport is nine times larger than La Guardia, New York has a special affection for the city's 'own' airport, which was built as a US domestic airport. The airport is built adjoining the East River.

La Guardia was the base of the world's first hourly, walk-on 'Air Shuttle' service, introduced by Eastern Airlines in 1960, using written-down Constellation airliners. Boeing 727s now fly the Shuttle.

passenger terminal was completed, costing $36 million. This was nearly seven times larger than the original 1939 terminal and provides 650,000sq ft of floor space. It consists of a four storey central section, two three-storey wings and four bi-level arcades leading to 36 aircraft gates. The first and second floor lobbies of the central section of the building have retail shops and consumer services, which include a hairdresser's, post office, bookstall, hobby shop and a drugstore. There is a completely equipped nursery, a conference centre and the La Guardia Terrace Restaurant.

Under the development scheme completed in 1964 the oval car park in front of the terminal building provided for parked cars on a single lower level. The pressure of space at the airport required that this car park be enlarged, however, and the one way this could be done was by constructing a multi-level structure on the site, and this was completed at the need of 1976, at a cost of $30 million, or slightly less than the cost of the complete terminal in 1964. The new car park houses 2,900 cars adjacent to the terminal; in total there are spaces for 6,000 cars at the airport.

La Guardia is also an important air cargo facility for US airlines, and air cargo warehouses at the airport provide 35,000sq ft of space.

A further important development became the subject of discussion at La Guardia in 1978, when one of the airport's prime users, Eastern Air Lines, contracted to buy 23 A300 Airbuses from Airbus Industrie of Toulouse. Buying these aircraft for its New York-Miami service, Eastern was presented with the problem of the aircraft being 8,000lb heavier in take-off weight than the airport's runway extensions could support. The airport was built originally in an era of flying-boats, and the runway extensions were constructed in 1967, and built on piers extending across the water in Flushing Bay. With the order of the European Airbuses by Eastern as positive, the Port Authority agreed to strengthen these runway extensions, at a cost of an estimated $850,000.

In 1982, 19 scheduled airlines were using La Guardia, and no fewer than 22 commuter airlines.

The elegant radial terminal pattern is a classic American concept and was chosen for New York's Newark in the 1960s. Newark has come into its own as a truly international hub in recent years, with the introduction of non-stop Newark-Gatwick flights.

Nice (Côte d'Azur)

France

Location: 3.5 miles SW of Nice
Elevation: 12ft (3.7m)
Runways in use: 1
05/23 9,840ft × 200ft (3,000m × 60m)
Passenger handled in 1981: 3,213,700
Total aircraft movements in 1981: 51,300
Cargo handled in 1981: 11,000 tonnes

Aviation history owes as much to Europe as it does to the USA, and some of Europe's earliest flying was done near the spot where a fine international airport stands today. It is known for example, that French pioneer aviator Captain Louis Ferber made flights with Lilienthal-type gliders at Nice, and in 1910, when aviation was well and truly launched, the town of Nice organised a grand aerial meeting for European aviators, at which prizes of up to Fr215,000 were offered, and at which records for both speed and altitude were established on aeroplanes like the Antoinette.

Then in 1920 the actual site of today's airport adopted the name of the California airfield because of the flying that was taking place there, and a 700m long grass runway was laid down. Sporting flying intensified at the airfield between 1922 and 1933. In 1936 the French company Potez Aéro-Service began a service between Nice and Toulouse and Bordeaux. The war interrupted continuance of this service.

The invasion of France by the Allies in 1944 saw the construction of a hard runway over 4,000ft long, and when the war finished in 1945 Air France installed an airline office with a view to commercial services. By 1949 the runway had been strengthened and lengthened to almost 6,000ft and air services were operating from Nice to London, Geneva, Tehran, Brazzaville and even Saigon. In 1955 the site was offically confirmed as that for the regional airport, and the airport was accorded the name Nice-Cote d'Azur.

By 1957 600,000 passengers a year were flying from Nice and it now looked very different from the sporting airfield of Captain Ferber's days and the enthusiasts of the California airfield. Nice-Cote d'Azur now sported an attractive little terminal, a cargo warehouse and well laid out car parks. By 1969, 12 years later, this terminal had been extended to accommodate travellers into the jet age, now spilling out of Air France's Caravelles and Boeing 707s, and the modest freight warehouse now stretched to long freight sheds equipped with mechanised handling devices. The car parks were becoming crowded for, as the hub of the French Riveria, Nice was now also the principal point of entry for tourists flying in from all parts of the globe. Indeed 'the blue coast' is fittingly named for tourist purposes, and the expansion of Nice airport and tourism in the region have gone hand-in-hand.

The single runway at the airport was further lengthened and improved and by 1973 stretched to 9,840ft (3,000m). The limits of its possible extension were being reached however, for Nice is a water-based airport, with its terminal right on the coast overlooking the Baie des Anges, and with its original

The water-based airport of Nice Cote d'Azur is being developed according to a grand plan for the whole region, which will eventually provide for a marine harbour created to the south of the runways, built on to the whole artificial land mass.

runway built on a strip of land literally within a few metres of the water. The beautiful location appeared to limit prospects for future development for big jets, but as airport planners have increasingly come to know, water can be as much of a friend to the landplane as it was to the flying-boat. In a dramatic decision in 1973 the French Secretary-General for Civil Aviation agreed in principle with the Nice Airport planners that a new runway could be added to the site, adjacent to the first, and built on land reclaimed from the sea and augmented by artificial filling. The runway capacity would therefore be completely doubled with this advanced plan and the prospect opened up for an eventual handling of 10 million passengers a year. In 1981 Nice handled 3,213,700 passengers.

The second runway was just one prime feature of a far-reaching airport development plan, which will see a complete redevelopment and modernisation of the whole airport, and which accords with a development plan for the Nice region. Amongst other things a future Port de Commerce is planned, with a harbour for ships incorporated in the land mass being developed to the south of the present and future runways, and which will thereby link land, sea and air facilities in one massive and remarkable complex.

Osaka International
Japan

Location: 4.7 miles from Osaka
Elevation: 39ft (12m)
Runways in use: 2
14L/32R 5,997ft×150ft (1,828m×45m)
14R/32L 9,842ft×200ft (3,000m×60m)
Passengers handled in 1981: 17,087,500
Total air transport movements in 1981: 128,300
Cargo handled in 1981: 216,500 tonnes

Osaka International Airport is located in a mountainous area, with approaches and take-offs made difficult by the mountain rises. The airport is also surrounded by industrial zones and housing, with houses reaching to within no less than 100m of the taxiway serving runway 32L. Because of this, strict noise abatement rules have had to be enforced, as some two million people have been affected by aircraft noise.

The airport was opened in March 1958 with a single runway, and the second runway, 14R/32L, was laid down in February 1970. There are separate domestic and international aprons, and a passenger terminal with four piers fitted with air bridges. There is also a cargo terminal with its own aircraft stands. The airport has been used by some 20 airlines, including Japan Air Lines and All Nippon Airways, the domestic operator.

By Western standards, the traffic using Osaka is very respectable, and because of this substantial traffic and also because of the noise problem and operational problems caused by the mountainous location, a new site for an airport to serve Osaka has been sought for many years. Plans going back to 1971 have proposed a new international airport built on land reclaimed from Osaka Bay. Then in 1977, the Japanese shipbuilding industry, at the Japanese Government's request, submitted to the Ministry of Transport plans for an off-shore airport comprising three floating structures in Osaka Bay, to be located some three miles south-west of the city. One structure would contain the terminal area and be linked to the shore by a bridge. The second structure, alongside the first and parallel with the shore, would provide a 13,000ft long runway. The third structure would provide connections to the mainland and airport supporting services.

Now it appears a new international airport called Kansai is to be built in Osaka Bay, off the Osaka suburb of Senshu. This is to be linked with the Shin-Osaka station by the bullet express train line. The Kansai airport project still appears to be in embryo rather than a project on which positive work has begun, and the Japanese Government in 1982 was said to be still lukewarm about the project. Meanwhile, Osaka International Airport is operating near saturation level.

Oslo (Fornebu)
Norway

Location: 5 miles from Oslo
Elevation: 52ft (16m)
Runways in use: 2
06/24 7,216ft×165ft (2,200m×50m)
01/19 5,740ft×165ft (1,750m×50m)
(Seaplane port also available)
Passengers handled in 1981: 4,256,000
Total aircraft movements in 1981: 65,800
Cargo handled in 1981: 26,900 tonnes

As with many Scandinavian airports, the capital city airport of Norway is under pressure because of the growth of traffic and because the geography of Norway places limits upon expansion of present sites.

An attractively situated airport, Oslo's Fornebu was planned and built by the city of Oslo and opened for traffic in June 1939. It is located about five miles from the heart of Oslo and surrounded by the sea on three sides.

The prewar life of the airport was brief, and during World War II the airport was used by the Germans for military purposes. It reopened for civil operations in February 1946, and since June 1947 has been owned and operated by the Norwegian Government, through the Civil Administration. It has been gradually enlarged, and a new passenger terminal was opened in 1964. This terminal has 10 aircraft gate positions.

The airport is served by 12 international and domestic airlines, and in 1981 over 4 million passengers used the airport. A development plan to increase the potential of Fornebu was submitted to the Norwegian Government in 1977. If a new airport for Oslo is built it may be at Hobö, about 19 miles to the south of Olso.

Oslo's Fornebu Airport is built near the water.

Palma de Mallorca   Majorca

Location: 4.3 miles east of city
Elevation: 13ft (4m)
Runways in use: 1
06L/24R 10,500ft × 150ft (3,200m × 45m)
Airport area: 1,300 acres
Passengers handled in 1981: 7,925,000
Total air transport movements in 1981: 71,300
Cargo handled in 1981: 26,000 tonnes

Palma Majorca must be regarded as one of the world's important airports by virtue of its very substantial annual traffic, almost equalising that of Zurich Airport in Switzerland. The explanation for this is, of course, tourism. Most of the passengers passing through the airport of Palma are holidaymakers, bound for the warm climate of Majorca through the medium of charter and inclusive tour flights.

The main airport for Majorca was for many years

Son Bonet, which had two grass runways, the longest of which was only 4,900ft. The Spanish Ministry of Transport therefore decided to develop the military aerodrome to the south-west, and this airfield, closer to the coast, became Palma de Mallorca. A scheduled service terminal was opened in 1966 and a new charter traffic terminal was opened in 1972. The two terminal aprons are joined together. The scheduled service terminal has some 13 departure and six arrival gates, and the charter terminal has six departure and six arrival gates and a total of 48 aircraft stands which is indicative of the large number of movements (which exceeded the number at Geneva annually).

Because of the buoyant traffic, Palma Airport is the subject of continued development work, and in the latest allocation of funds, the Spanish Ministry is earmarking further sums, for improvement work at Palma de Mallorca.

Paris (Orly/Charles de Gaulle)   France

ORLY
Location: 9 miles south of Paris
Elevation: 292ft (89m)
Runways in use: 4
07/25 11,972ft × 150ft (3,650m × 45m)
08/26 10,990ft × 150ft (3,320m × 45m)
02/20 7,870ft × 200ft (2,400m × 60m)
20/02 6,110ft × 200ft (1,865m × 60m)
Airport area: 3,750 acres
Passengers handled in 1981: 17,012,300
Total aircraft movements in 1981: 178,000
Cargo handled in 1981: 171,000 tonnes

CHARLES DE GAULLE
Location: 12 miles from Notre Dame, Paris
Elevation: 295ft (90m)
Runways in use: 1
11,800ft × 150ft (3,600m × 45m)
Airport area: 7,400 acres
Passengers handled in 1981: 10,935,700
Total aircraft movements in 1981: 102,000
Cargo handled in 1981: 447,300 tonnes

Aerogare (terminal) 2 at Paris's Charles de Gaulle Airport, with the departure lounge in the new facility.

It can be said fairly that the airports of Paris have always been important and they have always generally been magnificent too. From the time of the commencement of air transport services in 1919, Le Bourget played a part, after its initial start as a military grass airfield, and it went on to see the arrival of Charles Lindbergh on his solo transatlantic flight of May 1927 and then service as the principal airport for Paris right up to the time of the Jumbo jet age.

Even now Le Bourget functions, as a light aviation aerodrome and the site of the biennial Paris Air Show (Salon de l'Aéronautique et de l'Espace), while Orly Airport, to the south of the city, has taken on the role of secondary airport to the French capital and one at which a massive volume of traffic is handled annually. Orly, in fact, was assuming greater

importance even as the decision was taken to replace Le Bourget, and if its position today as the second airport for Paris appears misplaced, it is simply because the grand new facility of Charles de Gaulle Airport was planned right from the outset to become the major international hub for the French capital.

As of the moment, however, Orly Airport is by no means taking a back seat, for it is handling more traffic than CDG, and will doubtless continue to handle a heavy traffic until its facilities have to give way to the more expansive and far superior arrangements at the bigger new airport.

Orly was created on a plateau to the south of Paris and some six miles from the Porte d'Italie. It originally consisted of 629 acres of grassland, and in 1939 was made into a flying school for French Navy

Charles de Gaulle Airport, Paris, departed from an original plan featuring main, annular, terminal buildings served by surrounding satellite terminals, in favour of the elegant, if more conventional, elliptical terminal for its Aerogare 2, recently opened.

pilots. It was taken over by the Germans during the war, and in the first postwar year of 1946 was thought by the French Government to have potential for a future civil aerodrome. In 1949 this thinking was turned into a plan for action, and in 1954 basic studies were made for new works. These were initiated in 1957.

The new terminal buildings at Orly were opened in February 1961 by the President of the French Republic, General de Gaulle, who, as it happened, was to have his own airport memorial 13 years later in the form of the new airport at Roissy-en-France, just six miles north-east of Le Bourget.

The terminal structures today constitute two principal buildings, Orly-Sud and Orly-Ouest. Orly-Sud is a straight forward box-like structure stradding the main autoroute to the south, Route National No 7, and within this terminal are the usual multiplicity of passenger services, including an excellent hotel. The building has its own control tower for aircraft operations at the western end, and there are two piers with satellite holding lounges at either end, to the west and to the east.

Orly-Ouest is a much larger facility at the Orly site, with two extended pier terminals stretching from the main building and which between them provide parking stands for a dozen large aircraft, served by passenger bridges. This is the more recent development at Orly, and together with the Orly-Sud facility the whole complex combines to create an international airport which ranks among the busiest in Europe.

The later development in the Paris airport system has been Roissy, otherwise Charles de Gaulle Airport, which was opened for service on 13 March 1974. In looking for a site for this airport the planners of the Aeroport de Paris (Paris Airport Authority) were distinctly fortunate, for when they began research in 1957 it proved there was a region known as the Plain of Old France no more than 20km (12 miles) from Notre Dame, with land occupied by very few buildings. In the event, just one farm had to be demolished when construction work began in

1966, and even here a wood was left intact as it was skirted by the terminal roads. It is the PAA's intention ultimately to plant up to 50,000 trees on the site as part of a planned beautification programme to blend the airport into the landscape.

The location of the airport is near to the place known as Roissy-en-France, and for this reason it was originally called Roissy Airport, or otherwise Paris Nord. It was given the name Charles de Gaulle Airport in early 1974 at the time of the official opening.

In every sense this new Paris airport is grand and impressive. For a start the whole site covers 7,400 acres, which, while not totally occupied at the present, will doubtless be taken up by terminals, hangars, etc, by the end of the century when the airport is expected to reach saturation point. By that time, annual traffic is expected to be running at 50 million passengers.

In its present form Charles de Gaulle Airport can handle 12 million passengers a year. The first circular *Aerogare* is surrounded by seven wedge-shaped satellite terminals, each of which has parking provision for four wide-bodied aircraft. These satellite terminals are reached by a system of tunnels with moving walkways from the main terminal (the *Aerogare*) and which incorporates a four level multi-storey car park capable of accommodating about 4,000 cars. The 11-storey *Aerogare* is the principal terminal facility at CDG, and the original plan provided for the construction of five such buildings, with seven related satellites for each. A unique feature of CDG is its system of transport, which moves people about in the terminals by escalators and moving walkways, through a network of transparent tubes and passageways befitting an airport of the 21st century, let alone the 1980s. Charles de Gaulle Airport is in fact a rather breathtaking space-age airport for the visitor, and seen for the first time can be somewhat overpowering. For all that it is working well, and is in keeping with the era of the Concorde, which flies from the airport to New York every week.

The runway plan calls for four parallel runways, each of 11,800ft length (3,600m), but which may be extended to 13,800ft if necessary. The orientation of the first runway, which has been used since commencement of operations in March 1974, is east-west. The associated taxiways produce a total length of 46,000ft. As the high-speed taxiways are 200m (660ft) apart it has been possible to place a slow-speed taxiway between Them. There are almost two miles between Runways One and Two, and they are overlooked — as is the whole airport — by one of the world's tallest control towers, an 80m high (262ft) column with the elegantly shaped Navigation Centre at its base.

As traffic reached near-saturation point at CDG and with use of the first Aerogare, construction was started on a second terminal — Aerogare 2 — located in the south-east part of the airport. Scheduled to be fully operational in 1982, the terminal will handle mainly the traffic of Air France, and therefore was designed in close collaboration with the national airline. It departs from the circular concept of Aerogare 1, which was found to place

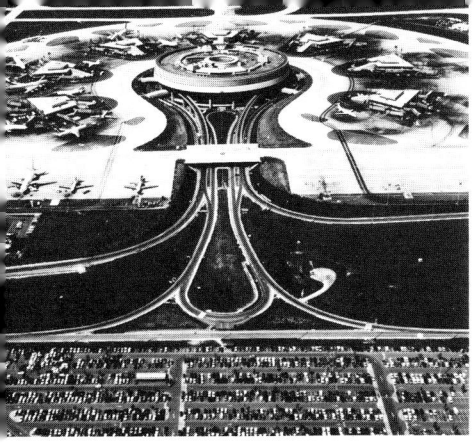

The main terminal at Charles de Gaulle, which was opened for service in 1974.

Aerogare 1 at Charles de Gaulle Airport is an 11-storey building, containing levels for car parking, passenger check-in, services, shops and restaurants.

constraints upon operators, and Aerogare 2 is rather more conventional in design, with elliptical layout. It will comprise some four modules in total, running in a direct line over the apron, each capable of handling an average annual traffic of five million passengers. The terminals are connected in pairs by a service road running parallel to an automobile viaduct.

The air terminal is positioned in the central area of the airport, between the already operational runway 1 and adjoining runway 2, which is still under construction. Aerogare 2 handles traffic only on one level, at approximately the height of the floor level of parking aircraft. Passengers cross the building, going through immigration formalities in the usual way, and move to their aircraft by way of passenger bridges. There are 12 to 16 parking stands in contact with the terminal. Adjoining the elliptical plan Aerogare 2 are associated administrative buildings, and there will be a central, underground car park capable of accommodating 5,000 vehicles.

Air France began using the terminal on 28 March 1982, calling it the 'Express Terminal' because the Aerogare is only 77 yards from the aircraft to the exit, thereby giving passengers a fast walk through the building. Luggage also has an express delivery procedure, because it is delivered by a simplified handling service.

Paris's second airport, Orly, still has more movements and more passengers than the city's principal airport, CDG. In foreground is the Orly-West terminal.

Peking (Beijing)

China

Location: 16 miles (25km) NE of city
Elevation: 115ft (35m)
Runways in use: 1
18R/36L 10,500ft × 165ft (3,200m × 50m)

The General Administration of Civil Aviation of China was established in 1962, and superseded the Civil Aviation Administration of China, also known as CAAC, and which was formed in November 1949 after the founding of the People's Republic of China. CAAC controls all civil aviation activities in China, including the administration of the airports in the country, of which Peking (Beijing) is the major one. CAAC is also the name of the national airline of the People's Republic of China, and which has a domestic network of over 170 routes and an international network linking China with 17 countries.

Peking is the hub of this air route network, and the growing number of overseas visitors to China will be impressed by the new terminal, which has many western-style features, and which together with the new runway was put into service in January 1980.

As the principal operator at Peking, the airline CAAC is serving a fast-expanding network with a growing fleet of increasingly modern aircraft. China has concluded air transport agreements with some 42 states worldwide, and the airline has interline arrangements with over 170 foreign carriers. Consequently, the aircraft fleet is getting bigger, and by necessity it is becoming more modern, to the degree that plans are already being made for the day when the airline can use on its routes aircraft made by the home manufacturing industry, which is currently in process of developing a Boeing 707-type, amongst others. The latest aircraft in the CAAC fleet are three Boeing 747SPs, and which have joined some 10 Boeing 707s, half a dozen Ilyushin Il-62s, fair numbers of Tridents, Viscounts, Il-18s, Antonov An-24s, and numerous smaller types, including Twin Otters and Bell 212 helicopters.

The three Boeing 747SPs are the flagship airliners of the fleet, and which CAAC fit to seat 291 passengers (including 18 first-class). The airline is now serving New York, San Francisco, Paris and Zurich, as well as London, and the 747SPs are the prime movers of passengers on inclusive tours and similar flights which devolve around the capital city airport of Beijing. China's recent move out into the world led to the acquisition of such aircraft, the inevitable follow-on of which was the requirement for new and modern airports like the new Peking.

Thus, at Peking airport today standard features are the familiar style passenger check-in desks, articulated passenger loading bridges, electronic message information boards, and satellite holding lounges, all of which are incorporated into the new Peking Airport, together with racetrack-type luggage conveyors in the baggage hall and moving walkways to transport passengers from the main terminal to distant waiting rooms. The restaurant in Beijing's main terminal is also comfortable enough by western standards, although we have no reports of the food. As might be expected, airport staff are numerous, while the ground handling equipment, including trucks, is not the most modern. Notably, however, much new ground handling equipment is coming into use, including scissor loaders and container transporters.

A revelation, perhaps, for western travellers, is the new Beijing Airport, serving Peking, capital city of the People's Republic of China. Note piers and airbridges.

Philadelphia International

USA

Location: 6 miles SW of city
Elevation: 23ft (7m)
Runways in use: 3
09L/27R 9,500ft×150ft (2,896m×45m)
09R/27L 10,500ft×200ft (3,200m×60m)
17/35 5,460ft×150ft (1,665m×45m)
Airport area: 2,300 acres
Passengers handled in 1981: 4,008,500
Total air transport movements in 1981: 255,600
Cargo handled in 1981: 93,300 tonnes

Philadelphia International has operated from its present location since 1940, although the first air activity on the site began in 1925. The city of Philadelphia provided 125 acres in the 1920s for the training of Pennsylvania National Guard pilots, and that former site is now a part of the airport's northeast corner. In 1930 the city of Philadelphia bought the adjoining Hog Island from the Federal Government to provide for airport expansion, but because of the Depression construction of the airfield and buildings did not begin until 1937. The aerodrome had been known since 1926 as the Municipal Aviation Landing Field, but the airport was officially opened on 20 June 1940 as Philadelphia Municipal Airport, and from that time American domestic airlines began using the airport, about 40,000 passengers being handled in the first year.

In 1953 a new terminal was built to handle the expanding traffic, and this was in use until 1973 when a new overseas terminal was erected. Further development work was made thereafter, and in 1977 the domestic area was appreciably expanded and four unit terminals constructed. This arrangement exists to the present day, and further plans are in hand for new development in accordance with traffic demands (passenger traffic actually fell by 6% in 1981).

Prague (Ruzyne)

Czechoslovakia

Location: 6.5 miles west of Prague
Elevation: 1,244ft (380m)
Runways in use: 3
31/13 10,660ft×150ft (3,250m×45m)
25/07 10,170ft×150ft (3,100m×45m)
22/04 7,515ft×200ft (2,300m×60m)
Airport area: 2,023 acres
Passengers handled in 1981: 1,603,000
Total aircraft movements in 1981: 36,500
Cargo handled in 1981: 7,300 tonnes

The contribution made to aviation by Eastern European countries over the years has been quite strong, and Czechoslovakia is no exception in this respect. The Zlin, Sokol and Aero ranges of light aeroplanes are an example of this contribution and they are enjoyed by pilots in various countries today.

Air transport first came to Czechoslovakia in 1920, when Air France began a service from Paris to Strasbourg and Prague, although the terminating aerodrome was not then Ruzyne but the military airfield at Kbely. The facility at Kbely served for 16 years as the airfield for both military and civil aircraft, and it was not until 1937 that a move was made to

Prague's Ruzyne Airport, where 82% of the passengers are international.

the plain of Ruzyne where a first airport was built. Air services from this new facility actually began on 1 March 1937, just 14 years after Czechoslovakia had been ranked among countries operating their own air services.

During the years between 1933 and 1937 the airport was given what were doubtless thought to be finishing touches to make it one of the best in Europe, and international recognition of this fact came in 1937 with an award of a gold medal for its construction by the Paris International Exhibition of Arts and Techniques.

The war terminated international air transport services at Prague, but the airport at Ruzyne had been positively established for the day when, in 1946, overseas links with Prague could be resumed. At this point a programme of modernisation was initiated covering the runway system, telecommunications and terminal building extensions. From this point on, development of the airport could not be carried out at a pace equal to the growth of air traffic — a story which has become familiar the world over. In 1937, Prague became a pace-setting airport, and 20 years later the state airline CSA was among the first ICAO member countries to move to the use of jet transports for scheduled services with the introduction of the Russian-built TU-104. Another 20 years on and Prague Airport was to see operations by the first supersonic airliner to fly the Tupolev Tu-144.

In the intervening years traffic has climbed in a manner which one might expect of one of the important airports in Europe, and from 1947, when 154,000 people passed through Prague Airport, the number of air transport passengers rose to 1,500,000 in 1967 and to 1.9 million in 1980. Aircraft movements are now in excess of 50,000 a year.

The terminal building was built to handle some four million passengers a year and a corresponding volume of cargo, mail and luggage. It is a steel and concrete skeleton with a steel roof covering, and topped by a 10-storey administrative block. The total floor area covered is five times more than that available at the original Ruzyne Airport.

By western standards the terminal complex is simple and modest in scope, with no system of complicated passenger channelling, but this is no fault, and the existing terminal facilities are pleasantly uncongested for travellers and offer comfort and repose. The terminal building has three quay galleries, two of which also serve as waiting rooms. They are designated at the eastern, western and northern galleries. The circumferential encasement of the building is made of aluminium and glass. Adjacent to the terminal building is the apron and which, prior to enlargement, was the size of Wenceslas Square, Prague.

Another prime building at Ruzyne is the CSA aircraft maintenance hangar. The airport is the headquarters base of Czechoslovak Airlines, which operates a dense domestic airline network, serving 10 key population centres in the country, as well as international services.

Rhodes (Paradissi)   Greece

Location: On the NE coast of Rhodes, 10 miles from the town
Elevation: 200ft (61m)
Runways in use: 1
10,824ft×150ft (3,300m×45m)
Passengers handled in 1981: 1,374,559
Total aircraft movements in 1979: 13,630
Cargo handled in 1981: 3,000 tonnes

The beautiful island of Rhodes, located in the Aegean Sea and just a few miles from the Turkish coast, was given Greece's best looking airport in 1977, when the new airport at Paradissi was opened during the summer.

Preliminary work on the planning of this airport, to replace the old airport at Maritsa, was begun in 1970, and the actual construction work started at the beginning of 1974. Over 40 airlines are now operating at the airport during the holiday season, and on peak days 13,000 passengers have been recorded on 60 flights, including four Jumbos. Paradissi is an airport well-fitted to serve this delightful holiday island, with its smart and spacious halls filtering the wonderful sunshine of the region.

The airport is not only new, but the terminal is the largest in Greece, approximately more than double in

Rhodes' Paradissi Airport opened in 1977.

size the terminals at Corfu and Heraklion, Crete. The passenger halls have a total surface area of over 75,000sq ft and the passenger terminals together have a total length of 820ft. The control tower is the tallest of all the Greek civil airports, at 105ft. At any one time up to 4,000 passengers and personnel can be accommodated in the terminal buildings.

Paradissi Airport was built to handle the increasing tourist traffic to Rhodes, which Maritsa was becoming unable to handle because of the limitations of the terrain which prevented further expansion. Rhodes has overtaken Thessalonika as the second busiest airport in Greece after Athens, and required enlarged facilities and a longer runway which could handle widebodied aircraft bringing large loads. The group of buildings comprises the main terminal, with two floors and a roof open for spectators and friends of departing passengers; the aircraft control tower building, housing ATC, telecommunications and related services, and a workshop building, which also houses quarters for the technical personnel. Passengers move through one-and-a-half levels, so there is no conflict of traffic nor any impediment of luggage movement. Departing passengers move to the first floor, while arriving passengers use only the ground floor.

The airport buildings are made of reinforced concrete, with faced pillars, and the arched shape of the side towards the town has been designed to give an appearance matching that of the architecture of the island. There are at the moment parking spaces for about 200 cars and 40 buses.

Rio de Janeiro (Galeao)   Brazil

Location: 8 miles NNW of Rio de Janeiro
Elevation: 16ft (5m)
Runways in use: 1
14/32 10,834ft × 150ft (3,300m × 45m)
09/27 13,120ft × 150ft (4,000m × 45m)
Passengers handled in 1980: 5,360,200
Total aircraft movements in 1980: 86,400
Cargo handled in 1980: 43,800 tonnes

The flight around the Eiffel Tower in October 1901 in a powered airship by the Brazilian Alberto Santos-Dumont serves as an illustration of the early interest in flying by the Brazilians, who have made notable strides in commercial aviation since then (Brazil's national airline VARIG is 52 years old). The beautiful city of Rio de Janeiro named its first airport after Santos-Dumont, and in more recent years the second airport at Galeao has been developed to become one of the world's most important airports.

Galeao is another of the world's water-based airports, and is located on the Rio coast almost in the shadow of the famed Sugarloaf Mountain. It is used by some four million travellers a year, and because of its traffic growth has required considerable enlargement.

Rio has been fortunate in that it has been possible to carry out this modernisation and expansion plan on the site of the existing airport, without recourse to the need to move elswhere. Long-time travellers to Rio are thus able to continue to fly to the existing site, with the difference that since spring 1977 they have flown to a new airport, which was eight years in the planning and construction.

The development of Rio Airport has been cleverly contrived to make use of the original runway and some existing facilities. There was one original runway and now there are two, and a third runway, parallel to the first, is planned. The new complex of four passenger terminals is located between the two runways and built on the site of some previous facilities. The best possible use is thus made of the land area available, and the life of the site extended for many years ahead — at least up to the year 2000.

The new plan features four terminal buildings, each in a half circle, facing each other in pairs and bisected by a roadway which distributes the traffic to the various buildings. This road system begins at the original Galeao roadway, and in the future will be connected on the opposite side to the mainland by means of express highways, which are planned by the State of Rio de Janeiro to form a traffic loop, with two airport entries and exits. The terminal buildings are based on the minimum-walking concept, whereby cars may be parked in the car park fronting the terminal, and left by their owners who proceed through the terminal to board waiting aircraft. The aircraft are parked around the airside of the terminal and reached by passenger loading bridges.

Under the design at Rio, arrival and departure flows take place on two levels, with completely independent accesses. After completing the usual travel formalities, departing passengers are directed towards large waiting areas on the upper level. Arriving passengers proceed through health and immigration channels at a mezzanine level between the departures and arrivals levels, and then move to baggage claim, from whence they proceed to the true arrivals level below. This brings them into the arrivals lounge, where they may be met by friends or relatives. On a higher level, and separated from the main passenger levels, are restaurants, bars, cafeteria, duty-free shops, a chapel and an a hotel, as well as telephones and post office facilities and a panoramic terrace.

An important characteristic of Rio's passenger terminal complex is its capacity for internal expansion. Whole areas have been left sterile within the building to be brought into use when needed. The car parking area, for example, which in 1978 occupied the ground level, can be increased by the addition of upper levels. The flexible planning is designed to guarantee a service life-term for each building of at least 20 years, and the possibility of multiplying the number of terminals, up to as many as eight, will guarantee the services of the entire airport beyond the year 2000. At the moment there is one half circular terminal. There will be four by 1990.

The existing runway and the new runway (09/27) form an open V and constitute a system which will

At Rio de Janeiro, probably one of the world's most beautiful airport settings, the airport of Galeao was modernised in 1977. The three-sector passenger terminal is served by double and single loading bridges.

be sufficient for traffic up to 1990. A third runway, laid parallel to the original strip, will raise the capacity of the airport further, and for operational needs beyond 2000. Runway 09/27 is over 13,000ft long and equipped for Category II operations. The apron areas cover over 3,000,000sq ft. The present terminal apron will provide 13 aircraft positions reached by telescoping bridges, and 19 remote parking positions. With four terminals in operation this number of parking positions will be multiplied accordingly. The terminal complex is overseen by a 184ft high control tower, located between Terminals One and Two, and equipped with the most modern aids including ILS, DME, VDF, VOR and primary and secondary radars.

Riyadh (King Khaled)   Saudi Arabia

Location: 5 miles NNE of city
Elevation: 2,050ft (625m)
Runways in use: 3
01/19 10,174ft×150ft (3,100m×45m)
11L/29R 9,836ft×150ft (2,998m×45m)
11R/29L 5,500ft×150ft (1,676m×45m)

The Kingdom of Saudi Arabia has been engaged in funding a massive airport programme, and the two prime airports at Jeddah and Riyadh have been notable beneficiaries of this remarkable programme. Plans for both Jeddah and Riyadh in particular have been remarkable by the style of airports built, and while Jeddah Airport is now in service, the new airport at Riyadh was in process of completion in 1982 but with official opening scheduled for 1983.

That airport, to be known as King Khaled International, will replace the existing airport of Riyadh International, located on the northern edge of the city, and which has been operating since the late 1940s, and from 1948 in particular when Saudi Arabian Airlines began scheduled operations. Saudi Arabian air transport got its start, in fact, when the President of the United States presented to HM the King of Saudi Arabia a DC-3, for the King's own use. In due course the King made this available to a newly constituted national airline, and some additional DC-3s were bought.

Since then and in the last 10 years in particular,

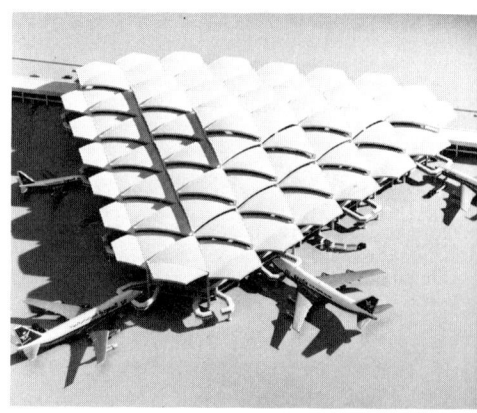

The new King Khaled airport at Riyadh, Saudi Arabia, will be another of the world's most distinctive airports, with its tent-like terminal structures.

Saudi Arabian air transport has seen a remarkable expansion, and the airline is now equipped with the latest TriStars and Boeing 747s, and has ordered 11 A300 Airbuses. In parallel with this development, the airports of the kingdom have been modernised extensively up to the present time, and Riyadh has been the subject of this work, with the first runway being joined by a second in 1956 and a third, parallel, runway in 1965. The first jets used by Saudia at Riyadh were Boeing 707s, and these were followed by Boeing 720Bs, which have still equipped the national airline.

The terminal complex at Riyadh also includes a VIP terminal and a Princes' Hall.

The new King Khaled International Airport is remarkable for its style, which features passenger terminals with canopied roofs made up of large individual panels, designed with the intention of harking back to tents of the desert. This original conception has been created with the many Moslem pilgrims of the Haj in mind, for many thousands of these pilgrims to Mecca pass through the airports every year. The concept also reflects the desert character of the Kingdom of Saudi Arabia.

There will be four triangular terminal modules with the 'sunshade' type roofs, and initial handling capacity of the King Khaled airport will be 10 million passengers. There will be two parallel runways initially, each 13,800ft long and 200ft wide (4,325m × 60m) and a third 10,500ft cross-wind runway.

Rome (Leonardo da Vinci Intercontinental)   Italy

Location: 23.8 miles SW of Rome
Elelation: 6.5ft (2m)
Runways in use: 3
16L/34R 12,790ft×200ft (3,900m×60m)
07/25 10,824ft×200ft (3,300m×60m)
16R/34L 12,790ft×200ft (3,900m×60m)
Airport area: 3,532 acres
Passengers handled in 1981: 10,921,100
Total air transport movements in 1981: 134,600
Cargo handled in 1981: 134,500 tonnes

Rome's intercontinental airport at Fiumicino adjoins the coastal town and front on to the Tyrrhenian sea. It was built to replace the previously used Ciampino Airport, and opened for international services in 1961. The plans were the work of the Ministry of Air Defence, while the airport was built by the Italian Ministry of Public Works. As the national airline, Alitalia had a hand in the planning of much of the terminal facilities. Then, as now, Rome's new airport had great potential for expansion because it was built on an extensive area of flat terrain, which was of course also important insofar as it presented no natural obstacles to flight.

Officially named Leonardo da Vinci Intercontinental, after the Italian aeronautical and mechanical genius of the 16th century, the airport was endowed with attractive contouring which did justice to some of the artistry of its namesake. The international building is, in essence, a large hall with a front walkway developing into natural piers on either side. Passengers reach the apron by means of short walkways and ramps projecting from the piers. The terminal hall is spacious, measuring 600ft×400ft, and the natural piers on either side are also very wide, with plenty of room for movement and waiting. The ramps from the piers lead down to the apron from where the traveller either walks to his waiting aircraft or takes an airside bus to the aircraft parking point. The weather at Rome usually guarantees that this is an acceptable procedure.

When first opened, the airport handled what was then regarded as the imposing figure of 2.5 million passengers a year. Over the years the traffic through

Rome's Fiumicino airport, otherwise Leonardo da Vinci, has had major terminal development recently. This is the international airside.

Leonardo da Vinci Interncontinental has swollen to 11.3 million passengers a year or over four times the original figure, and terminal extensions and additions have become increasingly necessary.

Aeroporti di Roma SpA, a corporation established by an Act of Parliament at the end of 1973 to take over the management of the two roman airports of Leonardo da Vinci-Fiumicino and G. B. Pastine-Ciampino, has set up a short and medium term expansion plan to adjust the airport of Fiumicino for present and future requirements.

The plan developed by Aeroporti di Roma provides for considerable expansion, and construction of a 'Y'-shaped pier equipped with loading-bridges, with 17 positions. The expansion plan covers also taxiways and the construction of multi storey car parking, the airport-town railway link, expansion of the road network, new cargo facilities and other works for general services.

The future plan for Rome's Leonardo de Vinci Airport is illustrated here, with the Y-shaped piers superimposed across the existing airport plan.

Aeroporti di Roma is now engaged in work to improve the efficiency of the existing facilities to meet the requirements of the passengers and airlines. The most recent of these is the construction of a new building for the in-flight catering service.

The new facility has a surface area of 9,000sq m — with 6,000sq m dedicated to production, meal preparation and washing up, while the other 3,000sq m are utilised for auxiliary services.

While located 24 miles to the south-west of Rome, Leonardo da Vinci is served by frequent airport bus services.

San Francisco International   USA

Location: 9.3 miles SE of city
Elevation: 10ft (3m)
Runways in use: 4
28R/10L 11,870ft×200ft (3,597m×61m)
28L/10R 10,600ft×200ft (3,212m×61m)
19L/1R 9,500ft×200ft (2,879m×61m)
19R/1L 7,000ft×200ft (2,121m×61m)
Airport area: 5,000 acres
Passengers handled in 1981: 20,840,009
Air transport movements in 1981: 262,600
Cargo tonnage handled in 1981: 318,000 tonnes

San Francisco International is now being served by some 35 carriers, including charter and third-level operators, and which scheduled airlines include the 'big names' in air transport such as British Airways, American Airlines, Delta, Eastern, Japan Air Lines, Lufthansa and CAAC, the airline of the People's Republic of China. San Francisco, in fact, is high on the list of the world's busiest airports, a position which has been steadily attained since the 1920s when aviation first 'took-off' in California.

SFO saw its first development in those early exciting days which saw the activity of as many seaplanes as land planes at San Francisco, because of the airport's unique location on the waterfront. The airport's complex of cruciform runways extends right into San Francisco Bay today, in fact, and the airport's two parallel runways 28R and 28L are built across the water, on land fill. A seaplane harbour is retained and used today at the south-west end of these runways. SFO airport has had problems with expansion, as so many airports have, partly because of this otherwise attractive location, and the problem of development has been overcome by redesigning the main 27-year old central terminal, the hub of airline activity at the airport. The central terminal complex has a number of pier terminals extending from the circular building complex, including the North and South Terminals and an International Rotunda, as well as the main, Central Terminal. The North and South Terminals are served by United Air Lines, Air Canada and Eastern, TWA, Northwest Orient, Mexicana and others, while between the South Terminal and the International Rotunda

operate overseas carriers such as Japan Air Lines, Qantas, Lufthansa and BA. Additional pier terminals serve other airlines, while the Central Terminal has been used by a number of operators, but which are now being relocated.

The relocation arises from the redesign of the Central Terminal itself, and which will now be called the International Terminal. This central structure will now be the home of international airlines previously operating from the South Terminal area, and which include the aforementioned JAL, Lufthansa, BA, etc. The Central Terminal has been rebuilt and new boarding area and Customs and Immigration facilities installed.

Existing departure piers have been replaced by a triangular-shaped boarding area connected to the International Terminal building. The new boarding area fits into the airport's long-term plan for the North, Central and South Terminals. The triangular configuration provides 10 gate positions to accommodate 10 B747s or DC-10s.

The rebuilding of this terminal, at a cost of $42 million, was considerably less than the cost of an entirely new terminal building, and it will do the job equally as efficiently. For overseas travellers, this will mean a new gateway point to San Francisco, and as the numbers of overseas visitors to San Francisco are increasing steadily each year, this new facility will be welcomed.

Passenger arrivals will be at first floor level, with departures on the second floor. Arriving passengers move downstairs from the gates to the international baggage claim area, Immigration and Customs. Departing passengers move from the new ticket and check-in departure hall, through a shopping concourse, and to the 11-gate boarding area. A spacious new arrivals hall has been incorporated for international passengers to meet welcoming parties.

One of the interesting features of San Francisco Airport is the safety precautions necessary against earthquakes, and this factor has been taken into account with the new Central Terminal. Safety measures include additional bracing in the terminal walls with reinforced steel columns, and the incorporation of sprinkler systems throughout the terminal.

Seattle International   USA

Location: 13 miles south of Seattle, 20 miles from Tacoma, Washington State
Elevation: 428ft (130m)
Runways in use: 2
16L/34R 11,900ft×150ft (3,660m×45m)
16R/34L 9,425ft×150ft (2,872m×45m)
Airport area: 2,100 acres
Passengers handled in 1980: 9,194,500
Total aircraft movements in 1980: 104,300
Cargo tonnage handled in 1980: 162,100 tonnes

In air transport circles Seattle, in Washington State, is noted for being the home of the mighty Boeing

company, and is so geared to aviation that all the local schools have courses in aeronautics.

Not surprisingly for this busy city, the international airport of Seattle-Tacoma, generally known as Sea-Tac, handles many aviation-orientated visitors among its annual throughput of more than seven million travellers, although as an important seaport and grain centre many of the visitors are on other business too.

Owned and operated by the Port of Seattle, authority to undertake airport activities was first granted in 1941, and land acquisition and the first airport construction work was started in 1942. While

Boeing had had its own aerodrome at Seattle for years, the civil airport did not actually commence airline operations until 1947, and then on the modest basis of 10 flights a day by two airlines. Today there are over 400 flights a day operated by 12 airlines.

The growth of traffic at Seattle-Tacoma has been very much a postwar surge and in particular in the last 10 years, when traffic has grown to such a degree that the airport now ranks among the top 24 airports world-wide in numbers of passengers annually passing through. This is, perhaps, one of the most significant things about Sea-Tac, although there are others, not the least of which was the introduction by the airport in 1972 of one of the first inter-terminal airport transit systems for passengers. Because of the recent growth, the Port of Seattle undertook a $175 million construction and re-modelling programme at the airport, and which was completed in 1973. Insofar as any airport construction programme is completed, this left Sea-Tac with a passenger handling capability for 12 million passengers annually. Eventually the airport expects to be handling efficiently 15 million travellers a year, which will place it among the busiest US airports.

The airport today is not beautiful but it is certainly functional and has a number of interesting features, one of which is the incorporation of two remote, satellite terminals, which passengers reach by underground passageway from the main building. These terminals have provision for parking of up to eight big aircraft around them, and support the operations from the piers on the north and south concourses. Their location on the apron, separate from the main building and in a 'sea' of concrete, also gives a clear taxying space for aircraft all around them, and eliminates the congestion of nose-in terminal parking at a main building. The arrangement also keeps down the noise level in the main terminal.

Seattle-Tacoma is an innovative airport, and amongst its innovations is the inter-terminal transit system (another has been the introduction of selected pieces of public art in the passenger terminals, which include Pacific Rim artefacts from the Burke Museum of the University of Washington). The Satellite Transit System consists of 9,050 feet of underground railway which connects the main passenger terminal with the north and south satellites. The system has two separate loops, the south loop beginning in the main terminal and end at the end of Concourse B, the pier projecting from the main terminal. En route, it serves the south satellite terminal. The north loop begins in the main terminal, makes stops at the north satellite terminal, and concludes at Concourse C, the northerly pier. There is also a shuttle beneath the main terminal wich connects the two loops.

As a 'people-moving' system, the Seat-Tac STS is said to be one of the most efficient in the USA, with a reliability factor of 99%. Made by Westinghouse Electric, the system has 12, 106-passenger vehicles running automatically over the network and serving eight stations altogether. The STS runs underground to free the aprons and surface for aircraft and ground support equipment, while providing a ready means of connection between the terminals for travellers. In 1976 these travellers numbered 9,304,984, or almost three million more passengers than used the airport on flights. The automatic operation is supervised by a central control computer, which controls station standing times and places the trains correctly in the system at all times.

Seattle-Tacoma Airport has its problems, not the least of which is warm fog, very prevalent in the region. This fog covers areas above the freezing point, and is more difficult to disperse than cold fog. In 1976 Sea-Tac suffered its worst fog season in 20 years, and as a way of dispersing it airlines at the airport carried out an intensified programme of fog seeding. This programme is maintained at the airport, but in October, November and December of the year seeding was done on 25 days altogether, and it was estimated that 289 carriers that might not have landed were able to do so as a result of the work. Category II ILS is installed at Sea-Tac. Another of the airport's problems has been aircraft noise, and Sea-Tac has been meeting this problem head-on with a relocation programme which, while costly, has been very successful, both for the residents of the area and the Port of Seattle. The programme began in 1975 with assistance provided by the Federal Aviation Administration under the ADAP plan (Airport Development Act Program), which enabled the Port to buy land along the airport perimeter from the owners at an independently appraised value. Once the owners were satisfied with the sums being offered, they began buying alternative accommodation and turned their properties over to the Port, which in most cases physically moved them from the area and smoothed and replanted the land. The programme has been continuing, along with other moves aimed at noise reduction.

These difficulties aside, Seattle-Tacoma intercontinental serves as an important traffic hub, provides employment for many thousands of people, and makes a profit for its operators.

Main terminal at Seattle-Tacoma, through which most of nine million passengers annually pass.

Singapore (Paya Lebar/Changi)

Singapore

PAYA LEBAR
Location: 7 miles east of the City of Singapore
Elevation: 66ft (20m)
Runways in use: 1
02/20 13,200ft×200ft (4,023m×60m)
Passengers handled in 1980: 6,291,800
Total aircraft movements in 1980: 68,200
Cargo handled in 1980: 181,800 tonnes

CHANGI
Location: On easterly tip of Singapore 16 miles from the city
Runways: 2
Parallel, 13,120ft×200ft (4,000m×60m)
11,000ft×200ft (3,355m×60m)
Airport area: 3,992 acres
Airport opened for traffic in July 1981
Passengers handled in 1981: 6,888,000
Total air transport movements in 1981: 64,100
Cargo handled in 1981: 187,000 tonnes

Singapore's new airport of Changi has spacious terminal halls for up to 30 million passengers by the end of the century.

The island of Singapore, in the South China Sea and just about a mile off the south end of the Malay Peninsula, is remarkable for the place it has earned in the world as a trading centre and international hub of business and commerce. Apart from the great progress the island republic has made in guiding its own destiny since independence in 1965, the former British Crown Colony has developed its trading and business skills to a fine art, and is now a world focal point for banking, insurance and currency exchange as well as a 'supermarket' for world goods. Some 59% of the products made in the Republic are exported, and the port of Singapore (one of the world's four busiest) is used by over 150 major shipping lines. Additionally, Singapore is one of the world's largest oil refining, blending and distributing centres, is a major world supplier of electronic components and a centre for shipbuilding and repairing.

The international airport has consequently become ever-more important to the country as this trading status has grown, and a rich variety of visitors on all kinds of missions is seen at the airport today. The traffic through the airport has literally soared, from 250,000 in 1958, to just under a million in 1966, to over 2.5 million in 1972, and to a remarkable five million just five years later, in 1977. Not surprisingly, the long-serving airport of Paya Lebar had to be replaced in 1980 by a brand new international airport at Changi, which is five times bigger than Paya Lebar.

The airport at Paya Lebar, located to the east on the island and seven miles from the city, was originally used by Britain as the principal Royal Air Force base in the Far East, but this role declined as the RAF's base at Changi was developed into an important military aerodrome. The operations at Paya Lebar gradually became almost entirely commercial, until a dozen airlines were using the airport in 1960 and big jet operations became routine.

Substantial development work took place in the early 1960s, and the hangars used by the military were modified and converted into a spacious passenger terminal. In time, travel facilities such as banking, postal and money exchanges were introduced, together with shops and a public restaurant. A new operations block was built in 1960, and in September 1961 the Area Control Centre was transferred to this permanent location. A new passenger terminal took its place alongside the operations block, and largely by a process of evolution, Paya Leba became a good international airport.

The single runway was lengthened steadily, from 8,000 to 9,000ft, then to 11,000ft and a further extension programme took it to the present 13,200ft, to make it among the longest in the world. Related threshold and apron improvement work was done, and an ILS installed.

The limits to expansion at Paya Lebar became clear in the early 1970s when the traffic was already doubling itself rapidly. The island of Singapore is only 26 miles long by 14 miles wide, and space is at a premium in this tiny republic. The only prospect for a widening of air transport facilities, therefore, was to look at the idea of a new airport site altogether, rather than trying to struggle along with the existing airport.

To be known as Changi International Airport, the new facility was formally approved by the Singapore Government in June 1975 and land reclamation for the airport began in April 1976. The airport location is partially on the site of the former RAF base, near the eastern tip of the island, but should be easier to reach by car than the present airport because two roads have been constructed specifically for the airport.

By the time of the opening of the first facilities, on 1 July 1981, passenger traffic at Singapore was running at about 6.2 million a year, and the first terminals at Changi will handle about 10 million passengers a year. Space is reserved for a second, third and fourth terminal should expansion be required by the end of the century, when annual

107

The work of international planners and construction companies which included the Dutch and Japanese, Changi Airport is equipped with 22 airbridges.

passenger throughput might be come 30 million passengers a year.

Much of the land that will be taken up by the new aiport has been reclaimed from the sea, and some is also former swampland. Appropriately enough, perhaps, a Dutch firm of airport planners and consultants (NACO) was responsible for the overall project, while the actual land reclamation work was undertaken by a Japanese firm of hydraulic engineers under the supervision of the Singapore Port Authority.

The principal terminal at Changi is a five-storey structure costing some S$250 million. It has two parallel fingers, each 1,900ft long. Work began on the foundations of this terminal in June 1977. The terminal — and its later fellows — will be equipped with moving walkways for passengers, new baggage conveyor systems, and airbridges for boarding the

aircraft from the terminal. In the first phase 22 airbridges have been installed and another eight later. In addition to these 30 aircraft stands near the terminal there are another 15 remoted stands. A hydrant fuelling system has been installed, and up to 80 aircraft movements an hour are possible.

There are two parallel runways, with the longest of 13,130ft (4,000m) length, based upon the military runway and lengthened from 2,500m. The new control tower and related ATC buildings is being built on what is known as Biggin Hill, and incorporates S$100 million of equipment. This includes radar capable of picking up supersonic aircraft at a range of over 200 miles.

In its first year of service, Changi International operated smoothly enough, bar the inevitable and occasional teething troubles, which produced little or no inconvenience to travellers. Some additional facilities were opened, and some modifications to the original plans were made. Singapore Airlines opened their S$63 million Engine Overhaul Centre in March 1982, but deferred, for the time being, construction of the Singapore Air Terminal Services (SATS) Transport Centre, which was designed to provide remote parking of ground support equipment. It was decided also, some time before the airport opening, to shelve the concept of air bridges for freighter aircraft at the massive Air Freight Terminal, which will have a processing capability for 570,000 tonnes of cargo a year.

The SIA Engine Overhaul Centre will enable the airline to save some S$30 million a year in engineering work, and also gain revenue from the execution of work for other airlines.

Changi International has now taken over from Paya Lebar Airport, but which hard-working old airport still has a function; airline crew training for SIA will still be carried on there for some time, and some flying may still be done.

Stockholm (Arlanda)   Sweden

Location: 25 miles from city centre
Elevation: 121ft (37m)
Runways in use: 2
01/19 10,800ft×150ft (3,273m×45m)
08/26 8,200ft×150ft (2,500m×45m)
Airport area: 7,700 acres
Passengers handled in 1981: 6,870,000
Total air transport movements in 1981: 116,800
Cargo handled in 1981: 54,500 tonnes

Until the early 1960s, Bromma was the capital city airport and the main airport for Sweden, and despite frequent pronouncements over its total closure, it is still used by commercial traffic today, and has been a prime hub for the domestic operations in Sweden of the home carrier Linjeflyg, which has used Fokker F28 Fellowships from the airport.

The main hub of commercial air traffic in Stockholm however is Arlanda International Airport, and Arlanda has the one disadvantage that it is some 40 minutes' bus ride away from the city, and which adds to travellers' overall journey time. The airport

had its first operational year in 1959-60, having been carved out of the virgin forest land of the Uppland countryside, and since then its traffic has progressively risen, to call for the construction of new terminal buildings and administrative facilities. Once at Arlanda, visitors do find an attractive and pleasantly-located airport of steel, glass and concrete in the heart of the country.

When it was first conceived in 1947, it was envisaged that Arlanda would be an airport for international traffic only, and mainly for long-distance flights. With the introduction of jets, and the noise problem resulting at Bromma, a fresh look was taken at the capabilities of Arlanda. The noise problem became unacceptable for Bromma, and so, step-by-step, different categories of traffic were moved to Arlanda. The first long-haul jets went to Arlanda in 1959, all scheduled international traffic in 1962, international charters in 1968 and most jet-powered domestic aircraft in 1969. It was decided in 1977 that the remaining domestic traffic should move to Arlanda, but Linjeflyg was given a 'stay of execution', and the company's aircraft have continued to use Bromma, partly as a result of improvements in the noise levels made to the aircraft in recent times.

Arlanda today has a complex of passenger terminals and aircraft hangars with a main international terminal, a separate domestic terminal and a base for charter operators. The main international terminal is a large wedge-shaped structure with passenger piers at either end of the wedge, and these are extended further across the apron by the attachment of passenger airbridges. The terminal is backed by a circular, covered car park, and by spacious open car parks behind that. A separate charter terminal has its own car park.

With an expectation of traffic at Arlanda reaching some 14 million passengers a year by 1990, the Swedish Board of Civil Aviation decided that a new international terminal would be required at the airport, and a go-ahead for the project was given by 1972. Construction work got underway at the end of 1973, and the terminal came into service in 1977.

The new terminal is a low building with a front made up of glass, stainless steel and concrete, and is 180m long. The two piers are 150m long each and 30m wide. Departing passengers enter the departure hall on the top floor by means of a ramp leading to the entrance hall; incoming passengers leave the aircraft and travel down escalators to the arrival hall on the ground floor. Road traffic to and from the terminal is on different levels.

Much thought was given to passenger comfort in the planning. Bearing in mind that most travellers have a fair amount of time on their hands during the time before embarking or in transit, the planners provided an observation deck on the roof of one pier, and a scenic view is obtained from the restaurant, cocktail bar and cafeteria, all of which are on the same floor. The restaurant and cafeteria together can serve 600 guests at one time. On either side of the entrance in the departure hall are offices of the various airlines and travel agents, and directly opposite are the check-in desks, with flap unit

Arlanda Airport will take over totally from Stockholm's old airport at Bromma during 1983. This is the newest international terminal.

departure information boards for identification purposes. These are matched by television screens and an information desk to keep passengers updated. Security and passport control points are at each end of the hall.

After check-in, passengers walk through security and passport controls into the pier where there are tax-free shops and a cafeteria. There are the usual facilities, such as washrooms, rest rooms and play rooms for children, with provision being made also for handicapped people. Embarkation is made by way of the covered airbridges directly to the aircraft.

Floor area of the international flight terminal is now 58,000sq m which compares with 10,000sq m of the old terminal. The airport is so arranged that the check-in desks for the left-hand pier are located to the left of the terminal, and right-hand desks serve the right-hand pier; passengers are categorised according to their flight.

Under the new arrangement there are places for 20 large aircraft around each of the piers, while there are additional remoted stands on the open apron.

Some 45 airlines are now using Stockholm Arlanda, 28 of which operate charter or inclusive tour services.

Sydney (Kingsford Smith)   Australia

Location: 4.3 miles south of city
Elevation: 6ft (2m)
Runways in use: 2
07/25 8,300ft×150ft (2,530m×45m)
16/34 13,000ft×150ft (3,962m×45m)
Airport area: 1,570 acres
Passengers handled in 1981: 8,222,100
Total air transport movements in 1981: 102,100
Cargo handled in 1981: 137,200 tonnes

Sydney is another of the water-based airports of the world, a runway extension into Botany Bay being made in 1975. Like Hong Kong, this gives Sydney Airport a particularly unique character.

Kingsford Smith Airport began life as a 160-acre grass aerodrome in the suburbs of Mascot, from which it took its original name. It was gradually expanded over the years until it became a three-

runway airport, sited within a bend of the Cooks River at the point where it enters Botany Bay.

A a principal airport for Australia, Kingsford Smith was required to meet the needs of postwar air traffic, and a reconstruction programme began in 1946. This involved diverting Cooks River into a new course over a mile long and 500ft wide. The old river course was filled in, and two new runways were built. New terminal and hangar blocks were erected and the airport equipped with new navigational aids.

When the jet age began runway 07/25 was extended, but the decision was taken also to extend runway 16/34 into Botany Bay, and land was reclaimed for the purpose. Subsequently, this runway was further extended to 13,000ft.

There are three separate terminal complexes at Sydney, a TAA terminal with seven departure gates and arrival channels, each fitted with an air bridge, a

separate terminal for Ansett operations with six departure and arrival gates, and having five air bridges, and an international three-level complex with 11 arrival and departure gates and seven air bridges. This arrangement was made to provide for the two major Australian domestic airlines, and to provide also for international flights.

In May 1970 a new international terminal was erected, and then a further development programme was put in hand, for new domestic and international

Sydney's main airport of Kingsford Smith is one of the most important in Australia, with a traffic throughput of over eight million passengers.

terminals, and which were brought into service in 1977. In terms of traffic Sydney is the major airport of Australia, and sees by far the greatest number of international and domestic travellers, with 2.4 million international passengers in 1981 compared with Melbourne's 961,000.

Taipei (Chiang Kai Shek International) Taiwan

Location: 25 miles from Taipei railway station
Elevation: 108ft (33m)
Runways: 5/23 First phase 12,000ft × 200ft (3,658m × 60m)
5R/23L Second phase 10,500ft × 200ft (3,200m × 60m)
Airport area: 2,965 acres
Passengers handled in 1981: 3,922,336
Total aircraft movements in 1980: 35,202
Cargo handled in 1981: 215,153 tonnes

The 250-mile long island of Taiwan, located 100 miles east of the Chinese mainland and previously known as Formosa, is still something of a political curiosity with its title of the 'Republic of China'. The country has, however, developed in the last few years to become one of the most commercially industrious on earth, and for this reason it already had two airports handling civil traffic and now has a third, brand new one.

Taipei is the capital city, with a population of over two million, and its airport is situated north-east of the city, approximately three miles from the centre. It

is the hub of air transport in the country, and handles over 180 domestic and international flights daily, with arriving and departing passengers averaging 10,000.

The Taipei International Airport Office was established in March 1950 under jurisdiction of the Civil Aeronautics Administration of the Ministry of Communications, and this office is responsible for the construction, operation and management of the airport. From 1965 air transport to and from Taiwan began to grow rapidly, and an enlargement and modernisation programme was put in hand to deal with the growing pressure on space. The annual growth rate of traffic was rising at an average of 21.8% or 6.5 times that of a decade before.

It is this sort of growth which led to the construction of a new airport to take the pressure from Taipei International, and this airport was completed in 1979, and opened for traffic on 26 February 1979. The new airport has been designed to handle traffic up to the year 2000. Like its predecessor, the airport is located in the north of the country, but rather further from the city, and is

The latest airport in Taipei serves Taiwan and was named after the Chinese nationalist leader Chiang Kai-Shek. This is the main terminal departure hall.

25 miles from Taipei railway station. A four-lane, five-mile long access road connects the airport with the TIA interchange of the freeway to the city, and makes for fast connection. The site of the airport is on a plain not far from the coast, on what was agricultural land. The site is known as Taoyuan, and has been named after the late President of the republic of Nationalist China.

The new airport covers almost 3,000 acres and has 10 operational areas, which can be categorised as aircraft operations, passenger terminal complex, control tower and flight operations, cargo terminal, aircraft maintenance, flight kitchen, fuel storage, airmail processing, telecommunications and airport hotel and administrative services. It will have two runways and a capability for handling 10 million passengers annually by 1990.

Taiwan's third airport is Kaohsiung International, which is to continue supporting the other two.

Sweeping lines of the new passenger terminal at Chiang Kai-Shek International.

Tokyo (Narita)   Japan

Location: Narita city, Chiba Prefecture, 41 miles east of Tokyo
Elevation: 135ft (41m)
Runways in use: 1
16R/34L 13,120ft×200ft (4,000m×60m)
Other runways:
16L/34R 8,200ft×200ft (2,500m×60m)
03/21 10,500ft×200ft (3,200m×60m)
Airport area: 2,630 acres
Passengers handled in 1980: 8,210,000
Total air transport movements in 1981: 63,900
Cargo handled in 1980: 431,000 tonnes

Probably no airport that has been constructed in the last few years received so much adverse publicity as did Narita Airport up to the time it was opened for flights in May 1978. The airport was built to serve Tokyo, although it is a good distance from the city (41 miles), a fact that has always been one of its less attractive features for passengers and airlines; however, it was political rather than air transport problems which gave the airport its bad name.

Narita was conceived in 1965 when the Japanese Ministry of Transport made an intensive investigation of 20 possible airport sites in the Tokyo area in the search for a replacement for Haneda. The island airport of Haneda, located in Tokyo Bay, had long ago been seen to be congested and with no potential for future development, and Narita finally emerged as the best possible replacement. In July 1966 the Japanese Government designated the Sanrizuka area of Narita city as the site for Tokyo's new airport. Narita is one of 36 cities in Chiba province.

Right from the start of the major construction work, which was commenced in 1970, Narita experienced opposition to its creation, firstly from environmental and pressure groups, but then later on an organised scale by hostile, anti-airport factions and political agitators, who claimed to speak for the world at large. For its part, the Tokyo International

Airport Corporation maintained that fear by local residents about safety and noise pollution could be dispelled, and that negotiations for the purchase of most of the private land required for the airport were satisfactorily settled by the original date set for opening. This was set for the beginning of 1974, but arguments over remaining pieces of land were amplified and exaggerated by political extremists to the degree that official opening of the new airport was delayed for four years.

Once open, however, Narita Airport offered modern facilities for both passengers and airline personnel. For passenger processing the airport has been designed with north and south wings to a main terminal building, the wings designed to function independently. The north wing is used by Japan Air Lines and a number of foreign airlines handled by JAL, and the south wing is used by other foreign airlines. Both wings have two separate satellite terminals with parking spaces for seven aircraft, to provide in total, parking places for 28 aircraft at one time. Each wing has separate inspection areas for immigration and customs formalities, while the central building houses restaurants, shops, offices and observation decks. Car parking places are also available, for up to 12,000 cars. The first and second floors in the terminals are designated for arriving passengers, while the third and fourth floors handle departing passengers. Priority was given to making this passenger flow smooth and without conflict. When Narita Airport was first planned, Haneda was already handling 4.5 million passengers a year and a replacement airport was considered vital by 1975. In 1976, because of the delays, the old airport was being obliged to handle almost 18 million

Narita Airport, Tokyo, which has replaced Haneda as main international airport, although Haneda is still eighth busiest in the world in passenger traffic.

While a long journey from the city, Narita is expected to have the journey time shortened by the introduction of faster train services.

bridge. They continue along the pier to the quarantine and immigration posts, and then downstairs to the baggage claim carousels. Departing passengers enter one of the wings of the terminal from a special approach road which leads to the kerbside entrance. They pass through ticket and baggage processing at one of the check-in islands and then proceed to the departure lobby, which commands a fine view of the aprons on the airside. The aircraft are reached by the passenger loading bridges.

In its first stage, Narita has two satellite terminals in use and one main runway, but it will ultimately have three runways, the longest being 13,120ft long. There will also be provision for an eventual 96 aircraft parking places. In its first stage Narita will handle 430,000 tonnes of cargo approximately; eventually it should have capacity for 1,400,000 tonnes a year.

Because of its great distance from the heart of Tokyo a number of systems of access were planned. These included an expressway and a high speed train service directly to the capital. The airport bus service runs between Tokyo City Air Terminal and the airport and takes about 80 minutes journey-time, depending upon the traffic. Railway trains run from north-east Tokyo to the Keisei Airport Station, which is a few hundred yards from the Narita Airport passenger terminal.

A high speed train service is also planned however, and this system, called HSST (High Speed Surface Transport) has been under development by Japan Air Lines, which has invested a great deal of its own money in research, a test track and the construction of several test vehicles to date. The HSST is powered by an electric linear induction motor, and which propels the vehicle along the track by magnetic levitation. In tests up to the middle of 1978 trains had reached speeds of over 180mph. Funding for this advanced project has been limited recently, and no progress has been made towards actual implementation of any passenger service.

passengers annually in wildly overcrowded conditions. In its first stages of development Narita was designed to handle up to 16 million passengers a year.

From the traffic projections it is clear that a new airport was necessary to handle the massive traffic passing through the Tokyo area, and the planners of the New Tokyo International Airport Corporation were determined to give careful attention to the matter of passenger processing. Apart from ensuring easy passenger access to any part of the buildings, even without signposting, they made psychological studies to determine behaviour patterns and emotional requirements of passengers and those accompanying them, and the results of these studies were employed in the architectural design of the terminal.

Arriving passengers enter the central hall of the appropriate satellite through a covered boarding

Toronto International (Malton)
Canada

Location: 17 miles from Toronto
Elevation: 569ft (173m)
Runways in use: 4
06L/24R 10,560ft×200ft (3,200m×60m)
06R/24L 9,500ft×200ft (2,895m×60m)
10/28 3,400ft×200ft (1,035m×60m)
Airport area: 14,000 acres
Passengers handled in 1981: 14,512,400
Total air transport movements in 1981: 198,000
Cargo handled in 1981: 181,000 tonnes

Canada has been placing increasing emphasis upon airport facilities in recent years, and recognition of the greater importance of airports has been manifeste in projects such as the new airport for Montreal at Mirabel, the decison to market Canadian airport planning and construction expertise in countries overseas, and the formation of airport

consultancy consortia able to offer to interested parties complete airports on a turnkey basis.

It was not always so. Canadian air transport really got under way only in the 1930s, and the important city of Toronto then had five relatively small grass airfields to handle the traffic. A larger airport became a requirement with the establishment of the government-sponsored Trans-Canada Air Lines (now Air Canada) in April 1937, and the first moves towards selecting a site for this airport were made in 1936. As T-CA was being given official blessing, the Department of Transport and the Toronto Harbour Commission were in process of deciding upon the site for Toronto's new airport, at Malton, 17 miles from the heart of the city and deep in Canadian farmland. The authorities could not know that 40 years later the Toronto area would generate the greatest number of air passenger trips among all metropolitan areas in Canada.

The first passenger terminal at Toronto Airport

113

was a converted farmouse, and this building served also as the administration centre, the operations hub and the weather office combined. It was to serve as a passenger terminal until 1939, when a new, wood-framed building was erected, and this in turn served, with various additions, until 1949.

The modern brick and steel terminal which took over was twice enlarged, to double both its length and width, before a problem arose which led to a completely fresh approach to providing for passengers. Simply, this problem was the growth in traffic, which has risen from 300,000 passengers in 1949 to 1,700,000 by the late 1950s. As improvisations were made to accommodate the passengers and the aircraft passenger walking distance grew from 300ft to 1,500ft and facilities grew ever more separated. Studies were commenced on the design for a new terminal in 1956, and the planning of this began in the autumn of 1957.

The structure which was to result was a building separated from the administration building and the airline workshops: it was as strikingly original airport terminal concept. Known as the Aeroquay, and today known as Terminal 1, the structure was a complete passenger terminal housing all facilities for travellers and nothing else. This included ticketing and processing areas, Customs halls, coffee shops and a restaurant, newstands and shops, spectators' galleries and a seven-storey car park with a capacity for 2,400 cars. Airport management functions and air traffic control were completely excluded from this bulding to leave the Aeroquay free for its intended purpose of serving as a passenger terminal. The facility was opened for use in February 1964, and cost $30 million.

The circular concept of the Aeroquay was designed to minimise passenger walking distances, to allow speed of service, provide protection from aircraft noise and offer convenient car parking facilities. In these aims the Aeroquay initially succeeded, for as a remoted facility placed in the centre of the apron, the terminal was removed from concentrated aircraft noise, and gave passengers ready access to the aircraft (by airbridges) and also to their cars, which they simply parked in the multi-storey box-shaped central core.

As airport authorities using island sites have come to discover, however, there are limitations on the practicalities of such designs in the fast-moving world of air transport, and Toronto Airport (now owned and operated by the federal government through the Canadian Air Transportation Administration) soon experienced problems. The first of these was the congestion caused by visitors to the airport in their cars. Sightseers caused exit delays from the car park of up to $2\frac{1}{2}$ hours, and clogged the access tunnels to the Aeroquay for airline travellers, thus reducing its effectiveness.

The number of passengers using the airport grew at a faster rate than anticipated and the airport operators were obliged to make modifications to the existing Aeroquay even before they were ready to construct another. Such a plan was in mind, dependent upon the success of Aeroquay 1. Originally designed to handle 3.2 million passengers annually, the Aeroquay has now been modified

The Aeroquay building at Toronto (foreground) has been joined by the rectangular Terminal 2, which allows easier expansion in accordance with traffic needs.

several times to increase its capacity to five million passengers annually. Serious overcrowding of passengers was experienced before long, and by 1970 it was clear there were insufficient gates for wide-bodied aircraft. The holding rooms were proving to be undersized for the task that would be required of them, and general limitations for future expansion were increasingly apparent with the Aeroquay concept.

The result of this was the reversion to linear type design by the planners when a second terminal, to be known as Terminal 2, was put into construction. This buildings is a straightforward rectangular structure adjoining the administration area and close to the airport approach roads, and embodying few, if any notable design features. In comparison with the Aeroquay it is depressingly dull, and it does have possibilities for expansion, and in this respect Terminal 2 will probably serve its purpose better than Terminal 1. It came into service first in June 1972, when Stage One was opened, and Stage Two was introduced into use in April 1973, when Air Canada transferred its entire operations from

Terminal 1. Stage Three in the terminal's construction was completed and fully operational in 1979. This stage comprised a 750ft extension to the east, housing international passenger processing facilities with nine additional gates and four passenger transfer vehicle loading docks. There is an adjoining five-level car park, for 5,300 cars.

Toronto International has four runways, an air cargo centre used by 80 different agencies, and a yearly throughput of aircraft which generate a total of 198,000 air transport movements.

In March 1981 plans were unveiled for a $28 million improvement programme for Terminal 1. This was followed by the announcement of a draft Master Plan for the whole airport, for development beyond 1990.

Toronto's newest terminal, Terminal 2, is seen in foreground here, backed by its car park facility. The Aeroquay terminal, at rear, incorporated car parking facilities and which caused some congestion problems in service.

Vancouver International Canada

Location: On Sea Island, 9 miles from Vancouver
Elevation: 9ft (2.7m)
Runways in use: 2
08/26 11,055ft×200ft (3,350m×61m)
12/30 7,400ft×200ft (2,240m×61m)
Airport area: 3,700 acres
Passengers handled in 1981: 7,097,992
Aircraft movements in 1981: 287,925
Cargo handled in 1981: 64,566 tonnes

1981 saw the 50th anniversary of Vancouver International Airport, a notable milestone for an airport which began, as so many did, with a flight by one enthusiast in the very early days of flying. The pilot who carved his name into Vancouver's airport

history was one Bill Templeton, who became the airport manager.

Templeton took-off in his home-built tractor biplane in 1911 from the grassy fields of Richmond's Minoru Park, and on that flight and subsequent flights noted the possibilities of Sea Island, a wide open tract which was flat and handy. After service in the Royal Canadian Naval Air Service during World War 1, Templeton became manager of Vancouver's 'official' airport which had been built on Lulu Island. To Templeton the Lulu Island site offered inferior landing facilities, which belief was confirmed when aviation pioneer Charles Lindbergh refused to land there for that reason. As airport manager, Templeton set about sponsoring in 1929 a by-law that enabled

Important western Canada airport, and home of airline CP Air, Vancouver International is the main airport for British Columbia.

Vancouver to purchase the site which he helped select, namely Sea Island. The 470-acre site of Sea Island proved to be an excellent choice, and two years later on 22 July 1931, the new Vancouver airport opened with Bill Templeton as its manager.

The Sea Island site was to offer much to air transport in the years to come, although that could hardly have been appreciated at the time. Sea Island, Vancouver, is totally flat, has obstruction free approaches, and substantial space available for expansion. In 1931 the entire airport staff consisted of three men and a horse and wagon. The horse and wagon was considered economical transport, however, as the horse grazed on the airport grass.

Vancouver's introduction to bigger league air transport came in July 1934, when United Air Lines commenced a trial service between Seattle and Vancouver, the first foreign terminal, served by the US airline. The service linked Vancouver by air with 200 cities served by UAL, and the experiment was so successful that by 1941 the frequency of the service had been increased by United to four a day.

In November 1936 the Canadian Department of

Bird's eye view of the traffic is presented by this scene from the Vancouver airport control tower.

Transport laid the guidelines for a nation wide air transport service, a feature of which was a federally-assisted airport construction programme, to which Ottawa contributed 25% of the costs. For Vancouver, this meant the laying of two paved runways, ramps and taxiways, the installation of a radio communication and meteorological service, and a component of the new national airport traffic control system.

1937 saw the birth of the state airline Trans-Canada Air Lines (later Air Canada), and the first route to be operated was Vancouver Seattle. In the same year Vancouver was connected by air to Prince George, Fort St John and Fort Nelson, and White Horse in the Yukon by Yukon Southern Air Transport. This airline was headed by Grant McConachie, who was later to be president of CP Air, for 18 years.

In 1941 a large Boeing aircraft factory was built at the airport, and engine and overhaul facilities were set up by aero engine firms for the war effort. Two new runways were built, together with additional hangars and office buildings. At the same time expansion of the south terminal was made and then accommodation provided for CP Air which began life in 1942.

In March 1946 the Federal authorities returned the airport to civic control, by which time the airport's value had become about $2 million. This was an already dramatic change from the $600,000 the site had cost the City Fathers in 1931. The name of the airport was officially changed in 1948 from Sea Island Airport to Vancouver International Airport, and one year later airport manager Templeton retired to hand over to a successor.

While T-CA and Canadian Pacific Air Lines (as CP Air was then known) were expanding dramatically at this time, CPAL established its headquarters at the airport, and has remained there ever since. The airline introduced a service to Hawaii, Canton Island, Fiji and Australia in 1949 giving the airport global status. A service over the North Pacific to Tokyo and Hong Kong followed in the same year. By 1956, the airport's statistics revealed the phenomenal traffic gains of the first 25 years; 771,632 passengers were handled at the airport. Further development followed steadily, and in 1981, the 50th anniversary year, over seven million passengers were handled at Vancouver International. Eleven airlines now serve the airport regularly, while the airport is also the base for numerous general aviation aircraft; a seaplane

base is a feature of the general aviation south terminal. There are now 10,000 people employed at the airport, with another 5,000 people employed in airport-related jobs.

The airport terminal is reached by Grant McConachie Way, which diverges at the approaches to Sea Island, and which divergent routes run from the island to Richmond and Vancouver. The rectangular terminal building has two Y-shaped ends, the two airside sections of which extend in the form of passenger piers and concourses across the apron. The terminal itself is a four-level structure with international arrivals and Customs and Immigration on the first level, domestic arrivals and US departures on level two, domestic and international departures on level three, and general offices, public facilities and airline first-class lounges on the uppermost level four. Shuttle bus services operate at regular intervals, while there are parking spaces for 2,500 cars.

By way of celebrating the first half century,

Vancouver International has drawn up a draft plan for the next 50 years. This provides for a $230 million expansion programme, allowing for an expanded passenger terminal, improved runways and numerous other innovations. Airfield improvements alone would absorb some $47 million of this sum. The plan provides for the construction of a third runway, north of the terminal, and a $37 million modification to the terminal building — which has been put in hand and is actually scheduled to be completed by 1983. An additional two-phase expansion of passenger handling facilities is scheduled to be completed by the late 1980s.

Additionally, 4,000 more car parking spaces will be provided, and a further passenger pier built across the airport apron, to add nine more aircraft gates to the existing 25. A further eight gates will be added with the construction of another wing built on to the terminal. By 1991 Vancouver International should be able to handle an expected traffic of 14 million passengers a year.

Vienna (Schwechat)   Austria

Location: 10.5 miles SE of Vienna
Elevation: 600ft (183m)
Runways in use: 2
12/30 9,840ft × 150ft (3,000m × 45m)
16/34 11,811ft × 150ft (3,600m × 45m)
Airport area: 2,346 acres
Passengers handled in 1981: 2,918,000
Total air transport movements in 1981: 55,700
Cargo handled in 1981: 35,700 tonnes

Vienna was amongst the first capitals in Europe to have regular air transport services, in the early 1920s, and the present site of Vienna Schwechat has been developed progressively to present a comfortable and efficient facility for the 2.8 million passengers that now use the airport annually. There are two airports serving Vienna (the other being Aspern), and Schwechat is the major international terminal, handling the services of some 27 airlines. While the facilities and aids have been brought right up to date, the airport buildings are of older design

and in the traditional architectural mould. Thus passenger buses are used to take travellers from the terminal to their aircraft, rather than airbridges or even projecting terminal piers.

The airport does have the facility of a railway line serving it, however, and recent work on the stations and related tunnels of this railway line has provided an efficient and impressive link between the airport and the city. It is now possible for travellers to reach the airport quickly by way of this line, and also to go directly to the passenger hall by way of tunnels from the roadway or car parks built for the airport. An autobahn runs past the airport, and a recent link road has been built as a spur from this autobahn to the terminal kerbside. The passenger is thus fairly well served at Vienna Schwechat with integrated road and rail facilities.

The picturesque location of Vienna Airport presents an attractive aspect to the arriving passenger. Note General Aviation base in foreground of picture.

Washington (Dulles International)   USA

Location: 27 miles west of Washington DC
Elevation: 313ft (95m)
Runways in use: 3
01L/19R 11,500ft×150ft (3,505m×45m)
01R/19L 11,500ft×150ft (3,505m×45m)
12/30 10,000ft×150ft (3,048m×45m)
Airport area: 10,000 acres
Passengers handled in 1981: 2,324,946
Total aircraft movements in 1981: 155,348
Cargo handled in 1981: 26,411 tonnes

For one of the world's most beautiful capital cities, it is fitting that Washington DC should have a beautiful airport, and Dulles International is the style of airport which has furthered the remarkable growth of air transport. Named after the former US Secretary of State, John Foster Dulles, the funds for the new airport were allocated in 1957, and construction work put in hand in September 1958. The airport was completed in November 1962 and officially opened before 50,000 spectators on 17 November 1962.

Before this, Washington National Airport had served the Federal capital since the mid-1940s. That airport still serves the region today and handled 13 million passengers in 1977, but Dulles International was created as the prime international airline facility, and the airport is established in that role today, although its traffic development has been disappointing so far and growing very little in the last decade.

Dulles is striking in many ways and its dramatic architecture is matched by impressive statistics. The airport covers twice as much ground as New York International, 10,000 acres, and is two-thirds the size of the city of Manhattan. It has one of the tallest control towers in the world, 193ft, and its construction involved the clearing of 1,200 acres of wooded land. When it was built on a specially selected site at Chantilly, Virginia, 27 miles west of the White House, a special access highway and a 14-mile long expressway had to be built for the sole purpose of providing a rapid connecting link between the airport and the city of Washington.

The terminal building was designed by the Finnish-born architect Eero Saarinen, who earned a reputation in air transport circles by his bizarre airport architectural creations. The terminal building rises from a base of approach ramps and has a concourse 600ft long and 200ft wide. There are no columns within the space. The hanging roof is supported by a row of columns 40ft apart on each side of the concourse, 60ft high on the approach side and 60ft high on the airfield side. The piers are likened to two rows of trees between which a continuous roof hammock has been hung. The roof is supported by light suspension bridge cables.

The control tower is similarly striking, and constitutes a concrete shaft rising from an observation platform with the control tower cab placed on top. A sphere surmounting the control tower cab houses airport surface detection radar.

Passenger procedures at Dulles are straightforward, with traffic flow taking place on two levels in the terminal. The carriage of passengers from the terminal to the aircraft was effected in a new and unusual way, however. This involved the use of 'Mobile Lounges', otherwise great upholstered coaches driven by engines at either end. An initial 21 of these mobile lounges was bought for Dulles, each carrying 102 people. This original fleet has since been enlarged with the introduction of 12 second-generation mobile lounges, known as the Plane-Mate, and which each carry 150 passengers. The Plane-Mates were designed to support the wide-bodied jets, and have a maximum speed of 19mph. As with their forerunners, the vehicles carry passengers directly from the terminal exits to the aircraft cabin doors, their doors mating with the side of the aircraft. The bodies of the vehicles are elevated to the required cabin door height by electrically-driven ball screw jacks. The maximum elevating height is 18.5ft.

In an expansion programme, the face of the terminal building at Washington's Dulles Airport (control tower side) was moved forward to increase terminal capacity.

Fifteen airlines are currently using Dulles, including five overseas airlines, British Airways, Air France, Pan American, TWA and Northwest Airlines. British Airways operate Concorde services to the airport from London.

In order to provide airline personnel with extra space for sorting baggage and to give another 50ft at the concourse level for passengers boarding and departing from the mobile lounges, a terminal widening contract took place, over 1978-80. This project involved the widening of the terminal along its entire length on the airfield side, adding approximately 75ft to the terminal's width at the

Deep in the heart of Virginia countryside lies the massive airport site of Dulles International, which was opened in 1962 specifically to serve as an international airport for the Federal Capitol.

ground level. Amongst other things this construction project provided a second roadway beneath the terminal to separate incoming and outgoing baggage.

If necessary, the terminal can be widened by another 300ft either side. A fourth runway may be built parallel to the third, 12/30.

Washington National   USA

Location: 3 miles from Washington DC
Elevation: 15ft (4.5m)
Runways in use: 3
03/21 4,724ft×150ft (1,440m×45m)
15/33 5,212ft×200ft (1,589m×60m)
18/36 6,870ft×200ft (2,094m×60m)
Passengers handled in 1981: 14,175,000
Total air transport movements in 1981: 193,500
Cargo handled in 1981: 20,100 tonnes

In spite of the fact that Dulles Airport was brought into service in 1962 to serve as a new and major airport for the capital, Washington National Airport continues to see a very heavy traffic, and indeed, a traffic far in excess of that of Dulles. Washington National Airport has served the Federal capitol since the mid-1940s, and it is perhaps not surprising that it sees such activity because of its close proximity to the capitol — it can be reached within a few minutes compared with the long ride to cover the 27 miles from Dulles.

The first airport serving Washington DC was Hoover Field, named after President Herbert Hoover, and which was opened in 1926. In 1927 another airport was opened near to Hoover Field, and in 1930 these two airports were merged into one. In September 1938 the first earthwork began on a new airport on a bend on the Potomac River, and this was to become Washington National Airport. The airport was opened for traffic in June 1941, with four runways, and since that time one runway has been closed.

The attractive and airy terminal was designed in Southern Colonial style, and while it has undergone major expansion over the years, this terminal is still used today. Various fingers were added, and in 1958 a north terminal was opened.

Washington National Airport is used essentially for US domestic operations today, with Dulles International being established as the Capitol's overseas airport.

Wellington International

New Zealand

Location: 5 miles SW of Wellington
Elevation: 37ft (11.5m)
Runways in use: 1
16/34 6,375ft×150ft (1,932m×45m)
Airport area: 230 acres
Passengers handled in 1981: 1,556,700
Total air transport movements in 1981: 44,300
Cargo handled in 1981: 38,900 tonnes

While Auckland is the largest city in New Zealand Wellington is the capital, and as such deserves its own airport. Both airports are located on the North Island but Wellington Airport is interestingly placed right on the edge of the sea, just near the Cook Strait on the southern tip of North Island.

When aviation first came to New Zealand, the British de Havilland aircraft company took its successful range of light aeroplanes to New Zealand and found the response promising enough to establish a branch of the company, de Havilland Aircraft New Zealand Ltd. The company flourished and developed its own flying facilities at Wellington, near its factory. As years passed, Wellington airfield was used more and more for air transport operations, and eventually a fully-fledged airport terminal was required. The de Haviland site was chosen by the Corporation of the City of Wellington for development into an airport proper, and air transport operations were gradually built up from the original de Havilland site.

A hard jet-age runway was required in due course, and the city Corporation decided that this should be built running right across the peninsula itself. This work was completed in 1961 and the result was an airport runway with a sea edge at both ends. The arrangement provided airliners with obstacle-free approaches, by virtue of the fact that landing aircraft came into Wellington over the sea. As a follow-on to this work, a new terminal, Customs hall and cargo centre were built, and civil aviation administration offices installed.

At the time of the 1960s development the air traffic control tower and its personnel were actually locted off the airport, situated on a knoll approximately 500ft north-west of the runway centre line, and surrounded by a large residential area. The tower building was located amongst private houses, and the aerodrome and approach control facilities provided from there. The arrangement worked well enough for the time.

The distance between the two islands is just 22 miles, and the transporting of bulk cargo was speeded by taking it across the straits by air rather than by sea, and Straits Air Freight Express carried on this air cargo operation with Bristol Freighter aircraft for many years, carrying cargo very much further in fact to Invercargill, at the extreme end of South Island.

Wellington Airport has undergone appreciable development since that time, and holds an even more important place in New Zealand's air transport operations today. Auckland is perhaps the more 'glamorous' airport, but Wellington Airport is the capital's own.

Wellington's international airport is a truly water-based airport, with the sea at either end. Evans Bay is at the near end, and Cook Strait at the other end of the runway.

Zurich (Kloten)

Switzerland

Location: 6 miles from Zurich
Elevation: 1,414ft (430m)
Runways in use: 3
14/32 10,824ft×200ft (3,300m×60m)
16/34 12,136ft×200ft (3,700m×60m)
10/28 7,500ft×200ft (2,500m×60m)
Airport area: 1,790 acres
Passengers handled in 1981: 7,973,300
Total air transport movements in 1981: 120,700
Cargo handled in 1981: 162,000 tonnes

In the Swiss airport system Zurich is the most important, serving as it does the country's principal city, and Kloten handles the bulk of the traffic. The airport at Kloten is, in air transport history terms, a young one, for sanction of the scheme for an airport and the necessary funds for its building were approved by the citizens of the Canton of Zurich in May 1946. Construction began that summer, and the west runway was opened on 14 June 1948. in November of the same year the instrument landing runway was opened, whereupon all commercial traffic was transferred from the airfield at Dubendorf to the new Kloten Airport, and Zurich's own airport was in business.

It was clear from the outset that the Canton of Zurich would be the owner and operator of the airport, and this situation prevailed until the semi-public Airport Real Estate Company was created to assume financial responsibility for the construction, maintenance and administration of the airport buildings, in particular the terminal buildings. Today, half of this company's shares are held by the Canton of Zurich together with the municipalities of Zurich,

Winterthur and Kloten and the Cantonal Bank of Zurich: the other half are privately held. The airport is run by Zurich Flughafen, the Zurich Airport Authority, while responsibility for air traffic control is held by Radio Suisse Ltd, a private company, operated under Federal supervision.

Since the commencement of operations in 1946, there have been a number of expansion schemes at Kloten, and one of the most important of these was begun in 1958, when the instrument runway was lengthened, the ramp was widened, and the airport lighting system substantially improved. Under this development scheme Swissair's technical base was expanded with the construction of a new hangar and workshop and an additional training school building. Finally, a new passenger terminal extension was made, which resulted in a trebling of surface area for passenger handling.

The next phase was the most important, and the people of the Canton of Zurich gave approval for this airport development programme even before the second stage development work had been completed. The heart of this development programme was the construction of a third runway (14/32) for instrument approaches. Apron extensions were also carried out to provide parking stands for some 45 aircraft, In addition, a new wide-bodied aircraft hangar was built, and a new access system to the airport. This last was most important, and included an underground railway link, between the

Kloten Airport, Zurich, is another example of an airport brought right up to date while essentially being on the same site for over 30 years.

airport and the city of Zurich. This has been integrated into the country's main east-west railway line.

Most important too, was the construction of a second passenger terminal, Terminal B, a three-storey second building with a finger dock. Arrivals, departures and transit levels in this terminal are directly connected to the pier, which has nine docking positions. Terminals A and B are connected by corridors in the domestic and transit areas.

Major airport for Switzerland, Zurich's recent terminal development work has included the incorporation of a rail link running right to the city.

A large scale development plan is in hand for the future, and this provides for a new pier with 13 parking positions, an Operations Centre, for aircrew enlargement of the apron and the construction of a new car park, to connect directly with terminal 'A'.

Index